God will bless *you*

God will bless you

Charles Spurgeon

Whitaker House

All Scripture quotations are taken from the *King James Version* (KJV) of the Bible.

GOD WILL BLESS YOU

ISBN: 0-88368-422-5
Printed in the United States of America
Copyright © 1997 by Whitaker House

Whitaker House
30 Hunt Valley Circle
New Kensington, PA 15068

Library of Congress Cataloging-in-Publication Data

Spurgeon, C. H. (Charles Haddon), 1834–1892.
    God will bless you / by Charles Spurgeon.
        p.   cm.
    ISBN 0-88368-422-5 (pbk.)
    1. Beatitudes—Criticism, interpretation, etc. 2. Spiritual life. I. Title.
BT382.S68 1997
241.5'3—dc21   97-38811

2 3 4 5 6 7 8 9 10 11 12 13 / 06 05 04 03 02 01 00 99 98

Contents

1

The Most Blessed Teaching

*And seeing the multitudes, he went up into a
mountain: and when he was set, his disciples came
unto him: and he opened his mouth, and taught them,
saying, Blessed are the poor in spirit: for theirs is the
kingdom of heaven. Blessed are they that mourn: for
they shall be comforted. Blessed are the meek: for they
shall inherit the earth. Blessed are they which do
hunger and thirst after righteousness: for they shall be
filled. Blessed are the merciful: for they shall obtain
mercy. Blessed are the pure in heart: for they shall see
God. Blessed are the peacemakers: for they shall be
called the children of God. Blessed are they which are
persecuted for righteousness' sake: for theirs is the
kingdom of heaven. Blessed are ye, when men shall
revile you, and persecute you, and shall say all manner
of evil against you falsely, for my sake. Rejoice, and be
exceeding glad: for great is your reward in heaven: for
so persecuted they the prophets which were before you.*
—Matthew 5:1–12

One enjoys a sermon all the better if he
knows something about the preacher. It is
natural that, like John in Patmos, we should
turn to see the voice that spoke to us (Rev. 1:9–12).
Turn here then, and learn that the Christ of God is
the Preacher of the Sermon on the Mount.

God Will Bless You

THE SERMON ON THE MOUNT

The Question Inherent in the Sermon

He who delivered the Beatitudes was not only the Prince of Preachers, but He was beyond all others qualified to discourse upon the subject that He had chosen. Jesus the Savior was best able to answer the question, "Who are the saved?" Being Himself the ever blessed Son of God and the channel of blessings, He was best able to inform us who indeed are the blessed of the Father. As Judge, it will be His office to divide the blessed from the accursed at the last, and therefore it is most fitting that in gospel majesty He should declare the principle of that judgment, so that all men may be forewarned.

Do not fall into the mistake of supposing that the opening verses of the Sermon on the Mount set forth how we are to be saved, or you may cause your soul to stumble. You will find the fullest light upon the matter of how to be saved in other parts of our Lord's teaching, but here He talks about the question, "Who are the saved?" or, "What are the marks and evidences of a work of grace in the soul?" Who should know the saved as well as the Savior does? The shepherd is the best one to discern his own sheep, and the Lord Himself alone infallibly knows those who are His. We may regard the marks here given of the blessed ones as being the sure witness of truth, for they are given by Him who cannot err, who cannot be deceived, and who, as their Redeemer, knows His own.

The Beatitudes derive much of their weight from the wisdom and glory of Him who pronounced them; therefore, your attention is called to this at the outset. Someone once said that "man is the mouth of creation, and Jesus is the mouth of humanity," but we prefer to think of Jesus as the mouth of Deity and to receive His every word as being encompassed with infinite power.

The Occasion of the Sermon

The occasion is noteworthy; the sermon was delivered when our Lord is described as *"seeing the multitudes."* He waited until the congregation around Him had reached its largest size and was most impressed with His miracles, and then He took the tide at its flood, as every wise man should. The sight of a vast crowd of people ought always to move us to pity, for it represents a mass of ignorance, sorrow, sin, and necessity, far too great for us to estimate. The Savior looked upon the people with an omniscient eye, which saw all their sad conditions. He saw the multitudes in an emphatic sense, and His soul was stirred within Him at the sight. His was not the transient tear of Xerxes when he thought on the death of his armed myriads, but it was practical sympathy for the hosts of mankind. No one cared for them; they were like sheep without a shepherd. Jesus therefore hastened to the rescue.

He noticed, no doubt, with pleasure, the eagerness of the crowd to hear, and this drew Him on to speak. A certain writer has well said, "Every man in his own trade or profession rejoices when he sees an opportunity of exercising it; the carpenter, if he sees a goodly tree, desires to have it felled, that he may employ his skill on it; and even so the preacher, when he sees a great congregation, his heart rejoices, and he is glad of the occasion to teach." If men become negligent of hearing, and the audience of a preacher dwindles down to a handful, it will be a great distress to him if he has to remember that, when many were eager to hear, he was not diligent to preach to them. He who will not reap when the fields are ripe for the harvest will only have himself to blame if in other seasons he is unable to fill his arms with sheaves. Opportunities should be promptly used whenever the Lord puts them in your way. It is good fishing where there are plenty of fish, and when the birds flock around the fowler, it is time for him to spread his nets.

The Place of the Sermon

The place from which these blessings were delivered is next worthy of notice: *"Seeing the multitudes, he went up into a mountain."* Whether or not the chosen mount was that which is now known as the Horns of Hattim is not a point that needs to be contested; that He ascended an elevation is enough for our purpose. Of course, He climbed upward mainly because of the accommodation that the open hillside would afford to the people. Also, the Preacher could readily sit down upon some jutting crag and still be both heard and seen.

I believe the chosen elevation of meeting also had its instruction. Exalted doctrine might well be symbolized by an ascent to the mount. A doctrine that could not be hid, and that would produce a church comparable to a city set on a hill, properly began to be proclaimed from a conspicuous height. A crypt or cavern would have been out of character for a message that is to be published upon the housetops and preached to every creature under heaven.

Besides, mountains have always been associated with distinct eras in the history of the people of God. Mount Sinai is sacred to the law, and Mount Zion is symbolic of the church. Calvary was also at the proper time to be connected with redemption, and the Mount of Olives with the ascension of our risen Lord. It was proper, therefore, that the opening of the Redeemer's ministry should be connected with a mount such as "the hill of the Beatitudes." It was from a mountain that God proclaimed the Law; it is on a mountain that Jesus expounds it. Thank God, it was not a mount around which boundaries had to be placed; it was not the mount that burned with fire, from which Israel retired in fear. It was, doubtless, a mount all carpeted with grass and dainty with fair flowers, upon whose side the olive and fig flourished in abundance, except where the rocks pushed upward through the sod and eagerly invited their Lord to honor them by making them His pulpit and throne.

I will also add that Jesus was in deep sympathy with nature, and therefore He delighted in an audience chamber whose floor was grass and whose roof was the blue sky. The open space was in keeping with His large heart, the breezes were akin to His free spirit, and the world around was full of symbols and parables, in accord with the truths He taught. Better than a long aisle, or tier on tier of a crowded gallery, was that grand hillside meeting place. If only we heard sermons amid soul-inspiring scenery more often! Surely preachers and hearers alike would be equally benefited by the change from the house made with hands to the God-made temple of nature.

The Posture of the Preacher

There was instruction in Jesus' posture: *"when he was set,"* He commenced to speak. I do not think that either weariness or the length of the discourse suggested His sitting down. He frequently stood when He preached at considerable length. I am inclined to believe that when He became a Pleader with sons of men, He stood with uplifted hands, eloquent from head to foot, entreating, beseeching, and exhorting, with every member of His body, as well as every faculty of His mind. However, now that He was, as it were, a Judge awarding the blessings of the kingdom or a King on His throne, separating His true subjects from foreigners, He sat down. As an authoritative Teacher, He officially occupied the chair of doctrine and spoke *ex cathedra,* as men say, as a Solomon acting as the master of assemblies or a Daniel coming to judgment.

He sat as a Refiner, and His word was like a fire. His posture is not accounted for by the fact that it was the Oriental custom for the teacher to sit and the pupil to stand, for our Lord was something more that a didactic teacher. He was a Preacher, a Prophet, a Pleader, and consequently, He adopted other attitudes when fulfilling those offices. But on this occasion, He sat in His place as Rabbi of the church, the authoritative Legislator of the kingdom of heaven, the Monarch in the midst of his people. Come here, then, and listen to the King in Jeshurun (Deut. 33:5), the Divine Lawgiver, delivering not the ten commands, but the seven, or, if you will, the nine Beatitudes of His blessed kingdom.

The Style of His Delivery

It is then added that *"he opened his mouth,"* and those who like to raise frivolous objections have said, "How could He teach without opening His mouth?" The reply to this is that He very frequently taught, and taught much, without saying a word, since His whole life was teaching, and His miracles and deeds of love were the lessons of a master instructor. It is not superfluous to say that *"he opened his mouth, and taught them,"* for He had taught them often when His mouth was closed. Besides that, we frequently meet preachers who seldom open their mouths; they hiss the everlasting Gospel through their teeth or mumble it within their mouths, as if they had never been commanded to *"Cry aloud, spare not"* (Isa. 58:1).

Jesus Christ spoke like a man in earnest. He enunciated clearly and spoke loudly. He lifted up His voice like a trumpet and published salvation far and wide like a man who had something to say that he desired his audience to hear and feel. Oh, that the very manner and voice of those who preach the Gospel would indicate their zeal for God and their love for souls! It should be so, but it is not so in all cases. When a man grows terribly earnest while speaking, his mouth appears to be enlarged, just as his heart is. This characteristic has been observed in vehement political orators, and the messengers of God should blush if the same thing does not happen to them.

"He opened his mouth, and taught them." Do we not have here a further hint that He here opened

His own mouth to inaugurate an even fuller revelation than He had from the earliest days when he opened the mouths of His holy prophets? If Moses spoke, who made Moses' mouth? If David sang, who opened David's lips so that he might show forth the praises of God? Who opened the mouths of the prophets? Was it not the Lord by His Spirit? Is it not therefore well said that now He opened His own mouth and spoke directly as the incarnate God to the children of men?

Now, by His own inherent power and inspiration, He began to speak, not through the mouth of Isaiah or Jeremiah, but by His own mouth. A spring of wisdom was now to be unsealed from which all generations would drink rejoicingly; now the most majestic and yet most simple of all discourses would be heard by mankind. The opening of the fount that flowed from the desert rock was not one half as full of joy to men.

Let our prayer be, "Lord, as You have opened your mouth, open our hearts," for when the Redeemer's mouth is open with blessings, and our hearts are open with desires, a glorious filling with all the fullness of God will be the result. Then also our mouths will be opened to show forth our Redeemer's praise.

THE BEATITUDES

Let us now consider the Beatitudes themselves, trusting that, by the help of God's Spirit, we may perceive their wealth of holy meaning. No words in the scope of the Holy Scriptures are more precious or more loaded with solemn meaning.

The Most Blessed Teaching

Blessed as Opposed to Cursed

The first word of our Lord's great standard sermon is *"Blessed."* The last word of the Old Testament is *"curse"* (Mal. 4:6), and it is meaningful that the opening sermon of our Lord's ministry commences with the word *"Blessed."* He did not begin in that manner and then change His tone immediately, for that charming word fell from His lips nine times in rapid succession. It has been well said that Christ's teaching might be summed up in two words, *believe* and *blessed*. Mark's gospel tells us that Jesus preached, saying, *"Repent ye, and believe the gospel"* (Mark 1:15), and in the passage before us, Matthew's gospel informs us that He came, saying, *"Blessed are the poor in spirit."* All His teaching was meant to bless the sons of men, for *"God sent not his Son into the world to condemn the world; but that the world through him might be saved"* (John 3:17).

> His hand no thunder bears,
> No terror clothes his brow,
> No bolts to drive our guilty souls
> To fiercer flames below.

His lips, like a honeycomb, drop sweetness; promises and blessings are the overflowings of His mouth. *"Grace is poured into thy lips"* (Ps. 45:2), said the psalmist, and consequently grace poured from His lips. He was blessed forever, and He continued to distribute blessings throughout the whole of His life until, as He blessed His followers, He was taken up into heaven (Acts 1:9). The Law had two mountains, Ebal and Gerizim, one for blessing and another for cursing, but the Lord Jesus blesses evermore and does not curse.

A Perfect Character, a Perfect Benediction

There are seven beatitudes that relate to character before us. The eighth is a benediction upon the persons described in the seven Beatitudes when their excellence has provoked the hostility of the wicked; and, therefore, it may be regarded as a confirming and summing up of the seven blessings that precede it. Setting the eighth aside, then, as a summary, I regard the Beatitudes as being seven and will speak of them as such. The whole seven describe a perfect character and make up a perfect benediction. Each blessing is precious separately, more precious than much fine gold. However, we will do well to regard them as a whole, for as a whole they were spoken, and from that point of view they are a wonderfully perfect chain of seven priceless links put together with such consummate art as only our heavenly Lord Jesus ever possessed.

No such instruction in the art of blessedness can be found anywhere else. The learned have collected two hundred and eighty-eight different opinions of the ancients with regard to happiness, and there is not one that hits the mark; but our Lord has, in a few telling sentences, told us all about it without using a solitary redundant word or allowing the slightest omission. The seven golden sentences are perfect as a whole, and each one occupies its appropriate place. Together they are a ladder of light, and each one is a step of purest sunshine.

The Most Blessed Teaching

Each One Rises above Those That Precede It

The first beatitude is by no means as elevated as the third, nor the third as the seventh. There is a great advance from the poor in spirit to the pure in heart and the peacemaker. I have said that the Beatitudes rise, but it would be quite as correct to say that they descend, for from the human point of view they do so. To mourn is a step below and yet above being poor in spirit, and the peacemaker, while the highest form of Christian, will find himself often called upon to take the lowest place for the sake of peace. The seven beatitudes mark deepening humiliation and growing exaltation. In proportion as men rise in the reception of the divine blessing, they sink in their own estimation and count it their honor to do the humblest works.

They Spring out of Each Other

It is as if each beatitude depended upon all that went before it. Each growth feeds a higher growth, and the seventh is the product of all the other six. The two blessings that we will have to consider first have this relation. *"Blessed are they that mourn"* grows out of *"Blessed are the poor in spirit."* Why do they mourn? They mourn because they are *"poor in spirit."* *"Blessed are the meek"* is a benediction that no man reaches until he has felt his spiritual poverty and mourned over it. *"Blessed are the merciful"* follows upon the blessing of the meek, because men do not acquire the forgiving, sympathetic, merciful spirit until they have been made meek by the experience of the first two benedictions. This same rising

17

and outgrowth may be seen in the whole seven. The stones are laid one upon the other in fair colors and are polished until they look like a palace. They are the natural sequel and completion of each other, even as the seven days of the world's first week were.

Each One Is Perfect in Itself

Notice, also, in this ladder of light, that though each step is above the other, and each step springs out of the other, each one is perfect and contains within itself a priceless and complete blessing. The very lowest of the blessed, namely, the poor in spirit, have their peculiar benediction, and indeed it is one of such an order that it is used in the summing up of all the rest. *"Theirs is the kingdom of heaven"* is both the first and the eighth benediction. Those who are of the highest character, namely, the peacemakers, who are called the children of God, are not said to be more than blessed. Undoubtedly, they enjoy more of the blessedness, but they do not possess more in the covenant provision.

The Blessing Is in the Present Tense

Note, also, with delight, that in every case the blessing is a happiness to be enjoyed and delighted in now. It is not "Blessed shall be," but *"Blessed are."* There is not one step in the whole divine experience of the believer, not one link in the wonderful chain of grace, in which there is a withdrawal of the divine smile or an absence of real happiness. Blessed is the first moment of the Christian life on earth, and blessed is the last. Blessed is the spark that trembles in the flax, and blessed is the flame that ascends to heaven in a holy ecstasy. Blessed is the bruised reed, and blessed is that tree of the Lord, which is full of sap, the cedar of Lebanon, which the Lord has planted. Blessed is the babe in grace, and blessed is the perfect man in Christ Jesus. As the Lord's mercy endures forever, in the same way will our blessedness endure.

The Blessing of Each One Is Appropriate

"Blessed are the poor in spirit" is appropriately connected with enrichment in the possession of a kingdom more glorious than all the thrones of earth. It is also most appropriate that those who mourn should be comforted; that the meek, who renounce all self-aggrandizement, should enjoy most of life, and so should inherit the earth. It is divinely fit that those who hunger and thirst for righteousness should be filled, and that those who show mercy to others should obtain it themselves. Who but the pure in heart should see the infinitely pure and holy God? And who but the peacemakers should be called the children of the God of peace?

Each One Is a Paradox

Yet the careful eye perceives that each benediction, though appropriate, is worded paradoxically. Jeremy Taylor said, "They are so many paradoxes and impossibilities reduced to reason." This is clearly seen in the first beatitude, for the poor in spirit are said to possess a kingdom. It is equally vivid in the collection as a whole, for it talks of happiness, and yet poverty leads the way and persecution brings up the rear. Poverty is the opposite of riches, and yet how rich are those who possess a kingdom! Persecution is supposed to destroy enjoyment, and yet it is here made a subject of rejoicing. See the sacred art of Him who spoke as never man spoke. At the same time, He can make His words both simple and paradoxical, and thereby win our attention and instruct our intellects. Such a Preacher deserves the most thoughtful of hearers.

All seven beatitudes composing this celestial ascent to the house of the Lord conduct believers to an elevated plateau upon which they dwell alone and are not counted among the world's people. Their holy separation from the world brings persecution upon them for righteousness' sake; in this they do not lose their happiness, but rather they have it increased to them and confirmed by the double repetition of the benediction. The hatred of man does not deprive the saint of the love of God; even those who revile him contribute to his blessedness. Who among us will be ashamed of the cross that must attend such a crown of loving-kindness and tender mercies? Whatever the curses of man may involve, they are so small a drawback to the consciousness of being blessed in a sevenfold manner by the Lord that they are not worthy to be compared with the grace that is already revealed in us.

2

Being Poor in Spirit

Blessed are the poor in spirit: for theirs is
the kingdom of heaven.
—Matthew 5:3

Bearing in mind from the preceding chapter the object of our Savior's discourse while teaching the Beatitudes, which was to describe the saved and not to declare the plan of salvation, we now come to consider the first of the Beatitudes: *"Blessed are the poor in spirit: for theirs is the kingdom of heaven."*

THE FIRST STEP

A ladder, if it is to be of any use, must have its first step near the ground, or feeble climbers will never be able to mount it. It would have been a grievous discouragement to struggling faith if the first blessing had been given to the pure in heart. The young beginner makes no claim to that excellence, while he can reach to poverty of spirit without going beyond his limit. If the Savior had said, "Blessed are the rich in grace," He would have spoken a great truth, but very few of us could have derived consolation from this.

21

God Will Bless You

Our Divine Instructor begins at the beginning, with the very ABCs of experience, and so enables the babes in grace to learn of Him. If He had started with higher attainments, He would have left the little ones behind. A gigantic step at the bottom of these sacred stairs would have effectually prevented many from trying to ascend, but thousands are encouraged to attempt the heavenly way because they are encouraged by the lowly step, which bears the inscription, *"Blessed are the poor in spirit."*

Where Law Leaves Off

It is worthy of grateful note that this gospel blessing reaches down to the exact spot where the law leaves us when it has done for us the very best within its power or design. The utmost the law can accomplish for our fallen humanity is to lay bare our spiritual poverty and convince us of it. It cannot by any possibility enrich a man. Its greatest service is to tear away from him his fancied wealth of self-righteousness, show him his overwhelming indebtedness to God, and bring him down to the earth in self-despair. Like Moses, it leads us away from Goshen, conducts us into the wilderness, and brings us to the verge of an impassable stream; but it can do no more. Jesus, our Joshua, is needed to divide the Jordan and conduct us into the Promised Land. The law rips the attractive Babylon-like garment of our imaginary merits into ten pieces and proves our wedge of gold to be mere dross, and thus it leaves us naked and poor and miserable (Rev. 3:17). To this point Jesus descends; His full line of blessing comes up to the verge of destruction, rescues the lost, and enriches the poor. The Gospel is as full as it is free.

This first beatitude, though placed at a suitably low point where it may be reached by those who are in the earliest stages of grace, is nonetheless rich in blessing. The same word, *"Blessed,"* is used in the same sense at the beginning as at the end of the chain of beatitudes. The poor in spirit are as truly and emphatically blessed as the meek or the peacemakers. No hint is given as to lower degree or inferior measure, but, on the contrary, the very highest blessing, which is used in the tenth verse as the gathering up of all seven beatitudes, is ascribed to the first and lowest order of the blessed: *"theirs is the kingdom of heaven."* What more is said even of the coheirs with prophets and martyrs? What more indeed could be said than this?

The poor in spirit are lifted from the dunghill and set, not among hired servants in the field, but among princes in the kingdom. Blessed is that soul poverty of which the Lord Himself utters such good things. He sets much store by what the world holds in small estimation, for His judgment is the reverse of the foolish verdict of the proud. As Watson well observed,

> How poor are they that think themselves rich! How rich are they that see themselves to be poor! I call it the jewel of poverty. There be some paradoxes in religion which the world cannot understand; for a man to become a fool that he may be wise, to save his life by losing it, and to be made rich by being poor. Yet this poverty is to be striven for more than riches; under these rags is hid cloth of gold, and out of this carcass cometh honey.

God Will Bless You

A Matter of Experience

The cause for placing this beatitude first is found in the fact that it is first as a matter of experience. It is essential to the succeeding characters, underlies each one of them, and is the soil in which alone they can be produced. No man ever mourns before God until he is poor in spirit, and he does not become meek toward others until he has humble views of himself. Hungering and thirsting for righteousness are not possible to those who have high views of their own excellence, and mercy to those who offend is a grace too difficult for those who are unconscious of their own spiritual needs. Poverty in spirit is the porch of the temple of blessedness.

As a wise man never thinks of building up the walls of his house until he has first dug out the foundation, so no person who is skillful in divine things will hope to see any of the higher virtues where poverty of spirit is absent. Until we are emptied of self we cannot be filled with God. Stripping away must be worked in us before we can be clothed with the righteousness that is from heaven. Christ is never precious until we are poor in spirit. We must see our own lack before we can perceive His wealth. Pride blinds the eyes, and sincere humility must open them, or the beauties of Jesus will be forever hidden from us.

The narrow gate is not wide enough to allow that man to enter who is great in his own estimation. It is easier for a camel to go through the eye of a needle than for a man proud of his own spiritual riches to enter into the kingdom of heaven. Hence it is clear that the character described in connection with the first beatitude is essential to the production of those characters that follow after, and unless a man possesses it, he will look in vain to the hand of the Lord for favor. The proud are cursed; their pride alone secures for them the curse and shuts them out from divine regard: *"The proud he knoweth afar off"* (Ps. 138:6). The lowly in heart are blessed, for Jehovah always has a tender regard for them and their prayers.

Given in the Absence of Praiseworthy Qualities

It is worthy of double mention that this first blessing is given rather in the absence than in the presence of praiseworthy qualities. It is a blessing, not upon the man who is distinguished for this virtue or remarkable for that excellence, but upon him whose chief characteristic is that he confesses his own sad deficiencies. This is intentional in order that grace may be that much more manifestly seen to be grace indeed, casting its eye first, not upon purity, but upon poverty; not upon those who show mercy, but upon those who need mercy; not upon those who are called the children of God, but upon those who cry, "We are not worthy to be called Your children."

God wants nothing from us except our needs, and these furnish Him with room to display His bounty when He supplies them freely. It is from the worse and not from the better side of fallen man that the Lord wins glory for Himself. Not what I have, but what I do not have, is the first point of contact between my soul and God. The good may bring their goodness, but He declares that *"there is*

none righteous, no, not one" (Rom. 3:10). The pious
may offer their ceremonies, but He takes no delight
in all their rituals. The wise may present their in-
ventions, but He counts their wisdom to be folly. But
when the poor in spirit come to Him with their utter
destitution and distress, He accepts them at once,
and more so, He bows the heavens to bless them and
opens the storehouses of the covenant to satisfy
them. As the surgeon seeks for the sick, and as the
almsgiver looks for the poor, in the same way the
Savior seeks out those who need Him, and upon
them He exercises His divine office. Let every needy
sinner drink comfort from this well.

Refers to the Spirituality of the Christian Dispensation

We should not forget that this lowest note upon
the octave of the Beatitudes, this keynote of the
whole music, gives forth a certain sound as to the
spiritual emphasis of the Christian dispensation.
Its first blessing is allotted to a characteristic, not
of the outer, but of the inner man; to a state of
soul, and not to a posture of body; to the poor in
spirit, and not to the exact in ritual. That word
spirit is one of the key words of the gospel dispensation. Garments, rituals, sacrifices, and the like
are ignored, and the Lord's eye of favor rests only
upon broken hearts and spirits humbled before
Him. Even mental endowments are left in the cold
shade, and the spirit is made to lead the caravan.
The spirit, the true man, is regarded, and all that is
left besides is of comparatively little worth. This
teaches us to mind, above all things, those matters
that concern our spirits.

Being Poor in Spirit

We must not be satisfied with external religion. If, in any ordinance, our spirit does not come into contact with the great *"Father of spirits"* (Heb. 12:9), we must not rest satisfied. Everything about our religion that is not heart work must be unsatisfactory to us. As men cannot live upon the chaff and the bran, but need the flour of the wheat, so we need something more than the form of godliness and the letter of truth. We require the secret meaning, the ingrafting of the Word into our spirits, the bringing of the brush of God into our inmost souls. All that is short of this is short of the blessing. The highest grade of outward religiousness is unblessed, but the very lowest form of spiritual grace is endowed with the kingdom of heaven.

It is better to be spiritual, even if our highest attainment is to be poor in spirit, rather than to remain carnal, even if in that carnality we could boast of perfection in the flesh. The least in grace is higher than the greatest in nature. Poverty of spirit in the publican was better than fullness of external excellence in the Pharisee. As the weakest and poorest man is nobler than the strongest of all the beasts of the field, so the lowliest spiritual man is more precious in the sight of the Lord than the most eminent of the self-sufficient children of men. The smallest diamond is worth more then the largest pebble; the lowest degree of grace excels the loftiest attainment of nature.

What do you say to this, beloved friend? Are you spiritual? At least, are you enough so to be poor in spirit? Does a spiritual realm exist for you, or are you locked up in the narrow region of things seen and heard? If the Holy Spirit has broken a door for you into the spiritual and unseen, then you are blessed, even if your only perception as yet is the painful discovery that you are poor in spirit. Jesus on the mount blesses you, and blessed you are.

WHAT FORMS THE CHARACTER?

Drawing still nearer to our text, we observe, first, that the person described in this beatitude has discovered a fact: he has ascertained his own spiritual poverty. This fact forms his character. Secondly, we observe that by this fact he is comforted, for he possesses *"the kingdom of heaven."*

An Old Truth

The person described in this beatitude always was spiritually poor. From his birth he was a pauper, and at his best, he is only a beggar. Naked, poor, and miserable (Rev. 3:17) is a fair summary of man's condition by nature. He lies covered with sores at the gates of mercy, having nothing of his own but sin, unable to dig and unwilling to beg, and therefore perishing in a poverty of the direst kind.

A Universal Fact

All men are by nature thus poor. In a clan or a family, there will usually be at least one person of substance, and in the poorest nation, there will be a few possessors of wealth. But alas for our humanity! Its whole store of excellence is spent, and its riches are utterly gone. Among us all, no remnant of good remains. The oil is spent from the jar, and the meal is exhausted from the barrel, and a famine is upon us, direr than what desolated Samaria of old. (See 1 Kings 17–18.) We owe *"ten thousand talents"* (Matt. 18:24), and have nothing with which to pay; even as much as a single penny of goodness we cannot find in all the treasuries of the nations.

A Deeply Humiliating Fact

A man may have no money, and yet his circumstances may involve no fault, and therefore no shame. However, our estate of poverty has this sting in it: that it is moral and spiritual and sinks us in blame and sin. To be poor in holiness, truth, faith, and love for God is disgraceful to us. Often the poor man hides his face as one who is greatly ashamed, yet we have far more cause to do so because we have spent our living riotously, wasted our Father's substance, and brought ourselves to lack and dishonor. Descriptions of our states that depict us as miserable are not complete unless they also declare us to be guilty. It is true that we are objects of pity, but we are much more objects of censure. A poor man may be nonetheless worthy of esteem in spite of the shabbiness of his apparel and the shortage of his provision, but spiritual poverty means fault, blameworthiness, shame, and sin. He who is poor in spirit is therefore a humbled man and is on the way to be numbered with those who mourn, of whom the second benediction says that *"they shall be comforted"* (Matt. 5:4).

A Little Known Fact

Most people are utterly ignorant about this matter. Though the truth about man's lost condition is

daily taught in our cities, few understand it. They
are not eager to know the meaning of a statement so
uncomfortable, so alarming. The bulk of those who
are aware of the doctrine and acknowledge that it is
scriptural still do not believe it, but put it out of
their thoughts and practically ignore it. "We see," is
the universal boast of the world's blind men. So, far
from realizing that they are destitute, the sons of
men are in their own estimation so richly endowed
that they thank God that they are not as other men.
No slavery is so degrading as that which makes a
man content with his servility. The poverty that
never aspires, but is content to continue in its rags
and filth, is poverty of the deepest kind, and such is
the spiritual condition of mankind.

A Spiritually Revealed Fact

Wherever the truth about our condition is truly
known, it has been spiritually revealed. We may say of
everyone who knows his soul poverty, *"Blessed art
thou, Simon* [son of Jonas]: *for flesh and blood hath
not revealed it unto thee"* (Matt. 16:17). To be spiritually poor is the condition of all men. To be poor in
spirit, or to know our spiritual poverty, is an attainment specially granted to the called and chosen. God's
omnipotent hand created us out of nothing, and the
same omnipotence is needed to bring us to feel that
we are nothing. We can never be saved unless we are
made alive by infinite power, and we cannot be made
alive at all unless that identical power first slays us. It
is amazing how much is needed to strip a man and to
put him in his true place. One would think that so
penniless a beggar must be aware of his poverty, but

he is not, and never will be, unless the eternal God convinces him of it.

Our imaginary goodness is more difficult to conquer than our actual sin. Man can sooner be cured of his sicknesses than be made to forego his boasts of health. Human weakness is a small obstacle to salvation compared with human strength; there lies the work and the difficulty. Hence, it is a sign of grace to know one's need of grace. He who knows and feels that he is in darkness has some light in his soul. The Lord Himself has worked a work of grace upon the spirit that is poor and needy and trembles at His Word. It is such a work that it bears within it the promise, even more so, the assurance of salvation; for the poor in spirit already possess the kingdom of heaven, and none have that but those who have eternal life.

One thing is certainly true of the man whose spirit knows its own poverty. He is in possession of one truth at least, whereas before he breathed the atmosphere of falsehood and knew nothing that he ought to know. However painful the result of poverty of spirit may be, it is the result of truth. With the foundation of truth being laid, other truth will be added, and the man will abide in the truth. All that others think they know concerning their own spiritual excellence is but a lie, and to be rich in lies is to be awfully poor. Carnal security, natural merit, and self-confidence, however much of false peace they may produce, are only forms of falsehood, deceiving the soul. But when a man finds out that he is by nature and practice "lost," he is no longer utterly a pauper as to truth. He possesses one precious thing at any rate; one coin minted by truth is in his hand.

For my own part, my constant prayer is that I may know the worst of my case, whatever the knowledge may cost me. I know that an accurate estimate of my own heart can never be anything but lowering to my self-esteem, but God forbid that I should be spared the humiliation that springs from the truth! The sweet apples of self-esteem are deadly poison; who would wish to be destroyed by them? The bitter fruits of self-knowledge are always healthy, especially if washed down with the waters of repentance and sweetened with a draught from the wells of salvation. He who loves his own soul will not despise them.

Blessed, according to our text, is the poor cast down one who knows his lost condition and is suitably impressed by it. He is but a beginner in wisdom's school, yet he is a disciple, and his Master encourages him with a benediction. More than that, He pronounces him as one of those to whom the kingdom of heaven is given.

Gaining Gospel Blessings

The position into which a clear knowledge of this one truth has brought the soul is one peculiarly advantageous for obtaining every gospel blessing. Poverty of spirit empties a man and so makes him ready to be filled. It exposes his wounds to the oil and wine of the good Physician. It lays the guilty sinner at the gate of mercy, or among those dying ones around the pool of Bethesda to whom Jesus is accustomed to come. Such a man opens his mouth, and the Lord fills it; he hungers, and the Lord satisfies him with good things (Ps. 103:5).

Being Poor in Spirit

Above all other evils, we have the most cause to dread our own fullness. The greatest unfitness for Christ is our own imaginary fitness. When we are utterly undone, we are near to being enriched with the riches of grace. Coming out of ourselves is next door to being in Christ. Where we end, mercy begins; or rather, mercy has begun, and mercy has already done much for us when we are at the end of our merit, our power, our wisdom, and our hope. The deeper the destitution the better:

> 'Tis perfect poverty alone
> That sets the soul at large;
> While we can call one mite our own
> We get no full discharge.

Should the heart be distressed because it cannot even sufficiently feel its own need, so much the better. The poverty of spirit is then just so much the greater, and the appeal to free grace all the more powerful. If we feel the need of a broken heart, we may come to Jesus for a broken heart, if we cannot come with a broken heart. If no kind or degree of good is perceptible, this is also but a clear proof of utter poverty, and in that condition we may dare to believe in the Lord Jesus. Though we are nothing, Christ is all. All that we need to begin with we must find in Him, just as surely as we must look to the identical source for our ultimate perfecting.

A man may be so misled as to make a merit out of his sense of sin, and he may dream of coming to Jesus clothed in a fitness of despair and unbelief. This is, however, the very opposite of the conduct of one who is poor in spirit, for he is poor in feelings as well as in everything else, and he dares no more commend himself on account of his humblings and despairings than on account of his sins themselves. He thinks himself to be a hardhearted sinner as he acknowledges the deep repentance that his offenses call for. He fears that he is a stranger to that sacred quickening that makes the conscience tender, and he dreads to, in any measure, be a hypocrite in the desires that he perceives to be in his soul. In fact, he does not dare to think of himself as anything other than poor, grievously poor, in whatever light he may be viewed in his relation to God and His righteous law.

Such a man who is poor in spirit hears of the humiliations of true penitents and wishes he had them. He reads the descriptions of repentance given in the Word of God and prays that he may realize them, but he sees nothing in himself upon which he can put his finger and say, "This, at least, is good. In me there dwells at least some one good thing." He is poor in spirit, and from him all boasting is cut off, once and for all. It is better to be in this condition than falsely to account oneself as a saint and sit in the chief places of the congregation. And moreover, it is such a safe position to occupy that he who is fullest of faith in God and joy in the Holy Spirit finds it adds to his peace to retain a full consciousness of the poverty of his natural state, and to let it run parallel with his persuasion of security and blessedness in Christ Jesus. Lord, keep me low; empty me more and more. Lay me in the dust; let me be dead and buried as to all that is of self, and then Jesus will live in me and reign in me and be truly my All in All!

It may seem to some to be a small matter to be poor in spirit. Let such persons remember that our

Lord places this gracious condition of heart so that it is the foundation stone of the celestial ascent of the Beatitudes, and who can deny that the steps that rise from it are sublime beyond measure? It is something inexpressibly desirable to be poor in spirit if this is the road to purity of heart and to the godlike character of the peacemaker. Who would not lay his head on Jacob's stone to enjoy Jacob's dream? Who would scorn the staff with which in poverty Jacob crossed the Jordan if he might but see the kingdom of heaven opened as the patriarch did? Welcome the poverty of Israel if it is a part of the conditions upon which we will receive the blessing of Israel's God. Instead of despising the poor in spirit, we would do well to regard them as possessing the dawn of spiritual life, the germ of all the graces, the initiative of perfection, the evidence of blessedness.

CHEERED AND BLESSED

Having discussed so far that the character of those who are poor in spirit is being formed by the knowledge of a fact, we now have to note that it is by a fact that they are cheered and rendered blessed: *"for theirs is the kingdom of heaven."*

The King Reigns over the Poor

It is not a promise about the future, but a declaration about the present; not "theirs shall be," but *"theirs is the kingdom of heaven."* The King of the heavenly kingdom is constantly represented as reigning over the poor. This truth is clearly revealed in many Scriptures. In the seventy-second Psalm,

David said, *"He shall judge the poor of the people, he shall save the children of the needy....He shall spare the poor and needy, and shall save the souls of the needy"* (v. 4, 13). As Jesus' virgin mother sang, *"He hath put down the mighty from their seats, and exalted them of low degree. He hath filled the hungry with good things; and the rich he hath sent empty away"* (Luke 1:52–53).

Those who enlist beneath the banner of the Son of David are like those of old who came to the son of Jesse in the cave of Adullam: *"Every one that was in distress, and every one that was in debt, and every one that was discontented, gathered themselves unto him; and he became a captain over them"* (1 Sam. 22:2). *"This man receiveth sinners, and eateth with them"* (Luke 15:2). His title was *"a friend of publicans and sinners"* (Matt. 11:19). *"Though he was rich, yet for your sakes he became poor"* (2 Cor. 8:9), and it is therefore proper that the poor should be gathered unto Him. Since Jesus had chosen the poor in spirit to be His subjects and said, *"Fear not, little flock; for it is your Father's good pleasure to give you the kingdom"* (Luke 12:32), we see how true it is that they are blessed.

Only the Poor in Spirit Will Endure

To the poor in spirit, Christ's rule is an easy yoke from which they have no wish to be released. To give God all the glory is no burden to them, and to cease from self is no hard command. The place of lowliness suits them; they count the service of humiliation an honor. They can say with the psalmist, *"Surely I have behaved and quieted myself, as a child that is weaned of his mother: my soul is even as a weaned child"* (Ps. 131:2). Self-denial and humility, which are main duties of Christ's kingdom, are easy only to those who are poor in spirit. A humble mind loves humble duties and is willing to kiss the least flower that grows in the valley of humiliation; but to others *"a fair show in the flesh"* (Gal. 6:12) is a great attraction, and self-exaltation the main object of life. Our Savior's declaration, *"Except ye be converted, and become as little children, ye shall not enter into the kingdom of heaven"* (Matt. 18:3), is an iron rule that shuts out all but the poor in spirit, but at the same time, it is a gate of pearl that admits all who are of that character.

Only the Spiritually Poor Will Value the Kingdom

The privileges of the kingdom are like pearls cast before swine to those who are not poor in spirit. The self-righteous care nothing for pardon, though it cost the Redeemer His life's blood; they have no desire for regeneration, though it is the greatest work of the Holy Spirit; and they set no store by sanctification, though it is the Father Himself who has made us suitable to be *"partakers of the inheritance of the saints in light"* (Col. 1:12). Evidently the blessings of the covenant were meant for the poor in spirit; there is not one blessing that would be valued by the Pharisee.

A robe of righteousness implies our nakedness; manna from heaven implies the lack of earthly bread. Salvation is vanity if men are in no danger, and mercy a mockery if they are not sinful. The charter of the church is written upon the supposition that it is formed of the poor and needy and is without meaning if it is not so. Poverty of spirit opens the eyes to see the preciousness of covenant blessings. As an old Puritan said,

> He that is poor in spirit is a Christ-admirer; he hath high thoughts of Christ, he sets a high value and appreciation upon Christ; he hides himself in Christ's wounds; he bathes himself in His blood; he wraps himself in His robe; he sees a spiritual dearth and famine at home, but he looks out to Christ, and cries, "Lord, show me Thyself, and it sufficeth."

Now, inasmuch as the Lord has made nothing in vain, since we find that the privileges of the gospel kingdom are only suitable to the poor in spirit, we may rest assured that for such they were prepared, and to such they belong.

The Poor in Spirit Reign as Kings unto God

The crown of this kingdom will not fit every head; in fact, it fits the brow of none but the poor in spirit. No proud man reigns; he is the slave of his boastings, the serf of his own loftiness. The ambitious worldling grasps after a kingdom, but he does not possess one. The humble in heart are content, and in that contentment they are made to reign. High spirits have no rest; only the lowly heart has peace. To know oneself is the way to self-conquest, and self-conquest is the grandest of all victories.

The world looks out for a lofty, ambitious, stern, self-sufficient man and says he bears himself like a king. Yet, in truth, the real kings among their peers are meek and lowly like the Lord of all, and in their unconsciousness of self lies the secret of their power. The kings among mankind, the happiest, the most powerful, the most honorable, will one day be seen to be, not the Alexanders, Caesars, and Napoleons, but the men akin to Him who washed the disciples' feet—those who in quietness lived for God and their fellowmen, unostentatious because conscious of their failures, unselfish because self was held in low esteem, humble and devout because their own spiritual poverty drove them out of themselves and led them to rest alone upon the Lord. The time will come when glitter and trinkets will go for what they are worth, and then the poor in spirit will be seen to have had the kingdom.

The Dominion Is Not Common

The dominion awarded by this beatitude to the poor in spirit is no common one; it is the kingdom of heaven, a heavenly dominion, far excelling anything that can be obtained this side of the stars. An ungodly world may reckon the poor in spirit to be contemptible, but God writes them down among His peers and princes. His judgment is true and far more to be esteemed than the opinions of men or even of angels. Only as we are poor in spirit do we have any evidence that heaven is ours; but having that mark of blessedness, all things are ours, whether *"things present, or things to come"* (1 Cor. 3:22).

All the security, honor, and happiness that the gospel kingdom is calculated to give upon earth belong to the poor in spirit; even here below they may eat of its dainties without question and revel in its delights without fear. Theirs also are the things not seen as yet, reserved for future revelation; theirs the second advent; theirs the glory; theirs the resurrection; theirs the beatific vision; theirs the eternal ecstasy. *"Poor in spirit"*—the words sound as if they described the owners of nothing, and yet they describe the inheritors of all things. Happy poverty!

Millionaires sink into insignificance, and the treasures of the Indies evaporate in smoke, while to the poor in spirit remains a boundless, endless, faultless kingdom, which renders them blessed, blessed forever, in the esteem of Him who is God over all. And all this is for the present life in which they mourn and need to be comforted, and in which they hunger and thirst and need to be filled; all this is for them while yet they are persecuted for righteousness' sake. What then must be their blessedness when they will *"shine forth as the sun in the kingdom of their Father"* (Matt. 13:43)? In them will the promise of their Master and Lord be fulfilled: *"To him that overcometh will I grant to sit with me in my throne, even as I also overcame, and am set down with my Father in his throne"* (Rev. 3:21).

3

Inheriting the Earth

Blessed are the meek: for they shall inherit the earth.
—Matthew 5:5

I have often reminded you that the Beatitudes in Matthew chapter five rise one above the other and spring out of one another, and that those that come before are always necessary to those that follow after. This third beatitude, *"Blessed are the meek,"* could not have stood first; it would have been quite out of place there.

When a man is converted, the first operation of the grace of God within his soul is to give him true poverty of spirit, so the first beatitude is, *"Blessed are the poor in spirit"* (Matt. 5:3). The Lord first makes us know our emptiness and so humbles us; next, He makes us mourn over the deficiencies that are so manifest in us. Then comes the second beatitude: *"Blessed are they that mourn"* (v. 4). First there is a true knowledge of ourselves, and then a sacred grief arises out of that knowledge.

Now, no man ever becomes truly meek, in the Christian sense of that word, until he first knows himself and then begins to mourn and lament that he is so far short of what he ought to be. Self-righteousness is never meek; the man who is proud

41

of himself will be quite sure to be hardhearted in his dealings with others. To reach this rung of the ladder of light, he must first set his feet upon the other two. There must be poverty of spirit and mourning of heart before there will come that gracious meekness of which our text speaks.

Note, too, that this third beatitude is of a higher order than the other two. There is something positive in it as to virtue. The first two are rather expressive of deficiency, but here there is a something supplied. A man is poor in spirit; that is, he feels that he lacks a thousand things that he ought to possess. The man mourns; that is, he laments over his state of spiritual poverty. But now there is something really given to him by the grace of God—not a negative quality, but a positive proof of the work of the Holy Spirit within his soul, so that he has become meek.

The first two characters that receive a benediction appear to be wrapped up in themselves. A man is poor in spirit—that relates to himself. A man's mourning is his own personal mourning that ends when he is comforted. However, the meekness has to do with other people. It is true that it has a relationship to God, but a man's meekness is especially toward his fellowmen. He is not simply meek within himself; his meekness is manifest in his dealings with others. You would not speak of a hermit, who never saw a fellow creature, as being meek; the only way in which you could prove whether he was meek would be to put him with those who would try his temper.

So then, this meekness is a virtue that is larger, more expansive, and works in a wider sphere than the first two characteristics that Christ has pronounced blessed. It is superior to the others, as it should be, since it grows out of them; yet, at the same time, as there is a fall parallel with the rise through the whole of the Beatitudes, so it is here. In the first case, the man was poor; that was low. In, the second case, the man was mourning; that also was low. But if he kept his mourning to himself, he might still seem great among his fellowmen. But now, he has come to be meek among them—lowly and humble in the midst of society—so that he is sinking lower and lower. Yet he is rising with spiritual exaltation, although he is sinking as to personal humiliation and so has become more truly gracious.

Now, having spoken of the connection of this beatitude, we will make two inquiries with the view of opening it up. They are these: first, who are the meek, and, secondly, how and in what sense can they be said to inherit the earth?

WHO ARE THE MEEK?

I have already said that they are those who have been made poor in spirit by God and who have been made to mourn before God and have been comforted; but here we learn that they are lowly and gentle in mind before God and before men. They are meek before God, and one Bible commentator divided that quality under two headings, namely, that they are submissive to His will and flexible to His Word. May these two very expressive qualities, as well as others that will also be discussed, be found in each one of us!

Those Who Are Submissive to God's Will

Whatever God wills, the truly meek will. They are of the mind of that shepherd on Salisbury Plain of whom a local doctor inquired, "What kind of weather will we have tomorrow?"

"Well," replied the shepherd, "we will have the sort of weather that pleases me."

The doctor then asked, "What do you mean?"

And the shepherd answered, "The weather that pleases God always pleases me."

"Shepherd," said the doctor, "your lot seems somewhat hard."

"Oh, no, sir!" he replied, "I don't think so, for it abounds with mercies."

"But you have to work very hard, do you not?"

"Yes," he answered, "there is a good deal of labor, but that is better than being lazy."

"But don't you have to endure many hardships?"

"Oh, yes, sir!" he said, "a great many; but then I don't have as many temptations as those people who live in the midst of towns, and I have more time for meditating upon my God. So I am perfectly satisfied that where God has placed me is the best position I could be in."

With such a happy, contented spirit as that, those who are meek do not quarrel with God. They do not talk, as some foolish people do, of having been born under a wrong planet and placed in circumstances unfavorable to their development. And even when they are struck by God's rod, they do not rebel against Him and call Him a hard Master. They are either silent and do not open their mouths because God has done it, or if they do speak, it is to ask for grace that the trial they are enduring may be sanctified to them, or they may even rise so high in grace as to glory in infirmities, so that the power of Christ may rest upon them (2 Cor. 12:9). The proudhearted may, if they will, accuse their Maker, and the man who is formed may say to Him who formed him, *"Why hast thou made me thus?"* (Rom. 9:20). But these men of grace will not do so. It is enough for them if God wills anything; if He wills it, so let it be—Solomon's throne or Job's dunghill. They desire to be equally happy wherever the Lord may place them, or however He may deal with them.

Those Who Are Flexible to God's Word

If the meek are really meek, they are always willing to bend. They do not imagine what the truth ought to be and then come to the Bible for texts to prove what they think should be there. Rather they go to the inspired Book with a candid mind, and they pray, with the psalmist, *"Open thou mine eyes, that I may behold wondrous things out of thy law"* (Ps. 119:18). When, in searching the Scriptures, they find deep mysteries that they cannot comprehend, they believe where they cannot understand. Where, sometimes, different parts of Scripture seem to conflict with one another, they leave the explanation to the great Interpreter who alone can make all plain. When they meet with doctrines that are contrary to their own notions and difficult for flesh and blood to receive, they yield themselves up to the Divine Spirit and pray, "What we do not know, teach to us."

When the meek in spirit find any precept in the Word of God, they seek to obey it at once. They do not quibble at it or ask if they can avoid it or raise that often repeated question, "Is it essential to salvation?" They are not so selfish that they would do nothing unless salvation depends upon it. They love their God so much that they desire to obey even the least command that He gives simply out of love for Him. The meek in spirit are like a photographer's sensitive camera, and as the Word of God passes before them, they desire to have its image imprinted upon their hearts. Their hearts are the fleshy tablets on which the mind of God is recorded. God is the Writer, and they become living epistles, written, not with ink, but with the finger of the living God. Thus are they meek toward God.

Those Who Are Humble

Meekness is a quality that also relates largely to our relationships with our fellowmen, and I think it means, first, that the person is humble. He bears himself among his fellowmen, not as a Caesar who, as Shakespeare wrote, does "bestride the narrow world like a Colossus," beneath whose huge legs ordinary men may walk and peep about to find themselves dishonorable graves, but he knows that he is only a man. He also knows that the best of men are but men at best, and he does not even claim to be one of the best of men. He knows himself to be *"less than the least of all saints"* (Eph. 3:8), and in some respects, the very chief of sinners (1 Tim. 1:15). Therefore, he does not expect to have the best position in the church leadership or the highest seat at the feast, but he is quite satisfied if he may pass among his fellowmen as a notable instance of the power of God's grace and may be known by them as one who is a great debtor to the loving-kindness of the Lord.

One who is meek does not set himself up to be a very superior being. If he is of noble birth, he does not boast of it; if he is born in the poorer class, he does not try to put himself on a level with those who are in a higher rank of life. He is not one who boasts of his wealth or of his talents; he knows that a man is not judged by God by any of those things. If the Lord is pleased to give him much grace and to make him very useful in His service, he only feels that he owes that much more to his Master and is the more responsible to Him. So he bows lower before God and walks more humbly among men.

The meek-spirited man is always of a humble temper and carriage. He is the very opposite of the proud man who, you feel, must be a person of consequence, at any rate to himself, and to whom you know that you must give way, unless you want to have an altercation with him. The proud man is a gentleman who expects to be a young man of fashion. He must always have his banner carried in front of him, and everybody else must pay respect to him. The great "I" stands conspicuous in him at all times. He lives in the first house on the street, in the best room, in the front parlor. When he wakes in the morning, he shakes hands with himself and congratulates himself upon being such a fine fellow as he is! That is the very opposite of being meek; therefore, humility, although it is not all that there is in meekness, is one of the chief characteristics of it.

Those Who Are Gentle

Out of this grows gentleness of spirit. The meek man is gentle; he does not speak harshly, his tones are not imperious, his spirit is not domineering. He will often give up what he thinks to be lawful, because he does not think it is expedient for the good of others. He seeks to be a true brother among his fellowmen, thinks himself most honored when he can be the doorkeeper of the house of the Lord (Ps. 84:10) or can perform any menial service for the household of faith.

I know some professing Christians who are very harsh and arrogant. You would not think of going to tell them your troubles; you could not open your heart to them. They do not seem to be able to come down to your level. They are up on a mountain, and they speak down to you as a poor creature far below them. That is not the true Christian spirit; that is not being meek. The Christian who is truly superior to others among whom he moves is just the man who lowers himself to the level of the lowest for the general good of all. He imitates his Master, who, though He was equal with God, *made himself of no reputation, and took upon him the form of a servant"* (Phil. 2:7). And in sequence, he is loved and trusted as his Maker was, and even little children come to him, and he does not repel them. He is gentle toward them, as a loving mother avoids all harshness in dealing with her children.

Those Who Are Patient

In addition to being humble and gentle, the meek are patient. They know *"it must needs be that offences come"* (Matt. 18:7), yet they are too meek either to give offense or to take offense. If others grieve them, they put up with it. They do not merely forgive seven times, but seventy times seven. In fact, they often do not feel as if anything had been done that needed any forgiveness, for they have not taken it as an affront.

They consider that a mistake was made, so they are not angry about it. A meek man may be angry for a moment—he would not be a man if he were not—but there is such a thing as being angry and yet not sinning (Eph. 4:26). And the meek man burns his anger wholly upon the evil and away from the person who did the wrong, and is as ready to do him a kindness as if he had never transgressed at all.

If there should be anybody reading this who is of an angry spirit, kindly take these remarks to heart, and try to mend that matter, for a Christian must get the better of an angry temper. Little pots soon boil over, and I have known some professing Christians who are such very little pots that the fire has made them boil over. When you never meant anything to hurt their feelings, they have been terribly hurt. The simplest remark has been taken as an insult and a meaning put upon things that never was intended, and they make their brothers offenders for a word or for half a word, and even for not saying a word.

Sometimes, if a man does not see such people on the street because he is nearsighted, they are sure he passed them on purpose and would not speak to them became they are not as well off as he is. Whether a thing is done or is left undone, it equally fails to please them. They are always on the alert for some cause of annoyance, and almost remind one of the Irishman at Donnybrook Fair, trailing his coat in the dirt and asking for somebody to tread on it so that he could have the pleasure of knocking that somebody down. When I hear of anybody like that losing his temper, I always pray that he may not find it again, for such tempers are best lost.

God Will Bless You

The meek-spirited man may be, naturally, very hot and fiery, but he has had grace given to him to keep his temper in subjection. He does not say, "That is my constitution, and I cannot help it," as so many do. God will never excuse us because of our constitutions. His grace is given to us to cure our evil constitutions and to kill our corruptions. We are not to spare any Amalekites because they are called innate sins, but we are to bring them all out, even Agag who came delicately (1 Sam. 15:32), and slay them before the Lord, who can make us more than conquerors over every sin, whether instinctive or otherwise.

Those Who Are Forgiving

But since this is a wicked world, and there are some men who will persecute us and others who will try to rob us of our rights and do us serious injury, the meek man goes beyond merely bearing what has to be borne, for he freely forgives the injury that is done to him. It is an evil sign when anyone refuses to forgive another. I have heard of a father saying that his child should never darken his door again. Does that father know that he can never enter heaven while he cherishes such a spirit as that? I have heard of someone saying, "I will never forgive So-and-so." Do you know that God will never hear your prayer for forgiveness until you forgive others? That is the very condition that Christ taught His disciples to present: *"Forgive us our debts, as we forgive our debtors"* (Matt. 6:12). If you take your brother by the throat because he owes you a dollar, can you think that God will forgive you the thousand dollars that you owe to Him?

50

So the meek-spirited man forgives those who wrong him. He reckons that injuries are permitted to be done to him as trials of his grace to see whether he can forgive them, and he does so, and does so quite heartily. It used to be said of Archbishop Cranmer, "Do my lord of Canterbury an ill turn, and he will be a friend to you as long as you live." That was a noble spirit, to take the man who had been his enemy and to make him to be a friend for all time. This is the way to imitate Him who prayed for His murderers, *"Father, forgive them; for they know not what they do"* (Luke 23:34), and this is the very opposite of a revengeful spirit. There are some who say that they have been wronged, and they will retaliate; but "retaliation" is not a Christian word. "Revenge" is not a word that ought to be found in a Christian's dictionary; he considers it to be of the Babylonian dialect and of the language of Satan. His only revenge is to heap coals of fire upon his adversary's head (Rom. 12:20) by doing this person all the good he can in return for the evil that the adversary has done.

Those Who Are Contented

The meek-spirited man is not ambitious; he is satisfied with what God provides for him. He does not say that his soul loathes the daily manna, and the water from the rock never loses its sweetness to his taste. His motto is, "God's providence is my inheritance." He has his ups and his downs, but he blesses the Lord that his God is a God of the hills and also of the valleys. If he can have God's face shining upon him, he cares little whether it is hills or valleys upon which he walks. He is content with what he has, and he says, "Enough is as good as a feast." Whatever happens to him, seeing that his times are in God's hand, it is well with him in the best and most emphatic sense.

The meek man is no Napoleon who will wade through human blood to reach a throne and shut the gates of mercy on mankind. The meek man is no miser, hoarding up with an all-devouring greed, everything that comes to his hand, and adding house to house and field to field, as long as he lives. The meek man has a laudable desire to make use of his God-given talents and to find for himself a position in which he may do more good to his fellowmen, but he is not unrestful, anxious, fretful, grieving, or grasping. He is contented and thankful.

Put those five qualities—humble, gentle, patient, forgiving, and contented—together with being submissive and flexible before God, and you have the truly meek man, the very opposite of the man who is proud, harsh, angry, revengeful, and ambitious. It is only the grace of God, as it works in us by the Holy Spirit, that can make us thus meek. There have been some who have thought themselves meek when they were not. The Fifth Monarchy men, in Cromwell's day, said that they were meek and that they were, therefore, to inherit the earth. So they wanted to turn other men out of their estates and houses so that they might have them, and thereby they proved that they were not meek. If they had been, they would have been content with what they had and let other people enjoy what belonged to them.

There are some people who are very gentle and meek as long as nobody tries them. We are all quite good-tempered while we have our own way, but the true meekness, which is a work of grace, will stand the fire of persecution and will endure the test of enmity, cruelty, and wrong, even as the meekness of Christ did upon the cross of Calvary.

HOW DO THE MEEK INHERIT THE EARTH?

Jesus said, *"Blessed are the meek: for they shall inherit the earth."* This promise is similar to the inspired declaration of Paul: *"Godliness is profitable unto all things, having promise of the life that now is, and of that which is to come"* (1 Tim. 4:8).

By Conquering the Earth

So, first, it is the meek man who inherits the earth, for he is the earth's conqueror. He is the conqueror of the world wherever he goes. William the Conqueror came to England with sword and fire, but the Christian conqueror wins his victories in a superior manner by the weapons of kindness and meekness.

In the Puritan times, there was an eminent and godly minister, Mr. Deering, who left some writings that are still valuable. While sitting down to eat one day, a graceless fellow insulted him by throwing a glass of beer in his face. The good man simply took his handkerchief, wiped his face, and went on eating his dinner. The man provoked him a second time by doing the same thing, and he even did it a third time with many oaths and blasphemy. Mr. Deering made no reply, but simply wiped his face. On the third occasion, the man came and fell at his feet, and said

God Will Bless You

that the demonstration of his Christian meekness
and the look of tender, pitying love that Mr. Deering
had cast upon him had quite subdued him. So the
good man was the conqueror of the bad one. No Alexander was ever greater than the man who could
bear such insults like that.

And holy Mr. Dodd, when he spoke to a man
who was swearing in the street, received a blow in
the mouth that knocked out two of his teeth. The
holy man wiped the blood from his face and said to
his assailant, "You may knock out all my teeth if you
will permit me just to speak to you so that your soul
may be saved," and the man was won by this Christian forbearance. It is wonderful what rough natures
will yield before gentle natures. After all, it is not
the strong who conquer, but the weak.

There has been a long enmity, as you know, between wolves and sheep. The sheep have never
taken to fighting, yet they have won the victory; and
there are more sheep than wolves in the world today. In England, the wolves are all dead, but the
sheep have multiplied by tens of thousands.

The anvil stands still while the hammer beats
upon it, but one anvil wears out many hammers.
Likewise, gentleness and patience will ultimately
win the day.

At this present moment, who is mightier—
Caesar with his legions or Christ with His cross? We
know who will be the victor before long—not Mu-
hammad with his sharp scimitar, but Christ with
His doctrine of love. When all earthly forces are
overthrown, Christ's kingdom will still stand.
Nothing is mightier than meekness, and it is the
meek who inherit the earth in that sense.

Inheriting the Earth

By Enjoying What They Have

If you find a man who thoroughly enjoys life, I will tell you at once that he is a meek, quiet-spirited man. Enjoyment of life does not consist in the possession of riches. There are many rich men who are utterly miserable, and there are many poor men who are equally miserable. You may have misery or you may have happiness in any condition of life, according to your state of heart.

The meek man is thankful, happy, and contented, and it is contentment that makes life enjoyable. It is so at our family meals. Here comes a man home to his dinner. He bows his head and says, "For what we are about to receive, the Lord make us truly thankful," and then opens his eyes and grumbles, "What! Cold mutton again?" His spirit is very different from that of the good old Christian who, when he reaches home, finds two herrings and two or three potatoes on the table, and he pronounces over them this blessing, "Heavenly Father, we thank You that You have ransacked both earth and sea to find us this feast." His dinner was not as good as the other man's, but he was content with it, and that made it better. Oh, the grumbling that some have, when rolling in wealth, and the enjoyment that others have, when they have but little, for the dinner of herbs is sweeter than the fatted calf if contentment is there (Prov. 15:17). *"A man's life consisteth not in the abundance of the things which he possesseth"* (Luke 12:15), but in the meek and quiet spirit that thanks God for whatever He pleases to give.

"Oh!" says someone, "but that is not inheriting the earth. It is only inheriting a part of it." Well, it is inheriting as much of it as we need, and there is a sense in which the meek do really inherit the whole earth. I have often felt, when I have been in a meek and quiet spirit, as if everything around belonged to me. I have toured a gentleman's estate, and I have been very much obliged to him for keeping the grounds in such order on purpose for me to walk through them. I have gone inside his house and have seen his picture gallery, and I have been very grateful to him for buying such grand pictures. I have hoped also that he would buy a few more so that I might see them when I came next time. I was very glad that I did not have to buy them and to pay the servants to watch over them, and that everything was done for me.

I have sometimes looked from a hill upon some far-reaching plain or some quiet village or some manufacturing town, crowded with houses and shops, and I have felt that they were all mine, although I did not have the trouble of collecting the rents that people perhaps might not like to pay. I had only to look upon it all as the sun shone upon it and then to look up to heaven and say, "My Father, this is all Yours, and, therefore, it is all mine; for I am an heir of God, and a joint-heir with Jesus Christ." (See Romans 8:17.) So, in this sense, the meek-spirited man inherits the whole earth.

By Being Glad of What Others Have

The meek-spirited man also inherits the earth in another sense, that is to say, whatever other men have, he is glad that they have it. Perhaps such a man is walking and gets weary; someone comes riding by, and he says to himself, "Thank God that man does not need to walk and get tired as I do. I am glad there is somebody who is free from that trial." He works very hard, and perhaps earns very little, but he lives next door to a workingman who earns twice his wages and says, "Thank God that my neighbor does not have such a pinch as I have. I should not like to see him in such a plight as I am in." Sometimes when I am ill, someone comes in and says, "I have been to see somebody who is worse than you are." I never get any comfort out of such a remark as that, and my usual answer is, "You have made me feel worse than I was before by telling me that there is somebody worse even than I am."

The greater comfort for a meek man is this: "Though I am ill, there are plenty of people who are well," or, "Though I am blind, I bless God that my dear friends can see the flowers and the sun," or, "Though I am lame, I am thankful that others can run," or, "Though I am depressed in spirit, I am glad that there are sweet-voiced singers," or, "Though I am an owl, I rejoice that there are larks to soar and sing, and eagles to mount toward the sun." The meek-spirited man is glad to know that other people are happy, and their happiness is his happiness. He will have a great number of heavens, for everybody else's heaven will be a heaven to him. It will be a heaven to him to know that so many other people are in heaven, and he will praise the Lord for each one whom he sees there. Meekness gives us the enjoyment of what is other people's, yet they do not have any less because of our enjoyment of it.

God Will Bless You

By Seeing the Good in Others

Again, the meek-spirited man inherits the earth in this sense: if there is anybody who is good anywhere near him, he is sure to see him. I have known people to join the church, and after they have been in it a little while, they have said, "There is no love there." Now, when a brother says, "There is no love there," I know that he has been looking in the glass, and that his own reflection has suggested his remark. Such persons cry out about the deceptions and hypocrisies in the professing church—and they have some cause for doing so—only it is a pity that they cannot also see the good people, the true saints, who are there. The Lord still has a people who love and fear Him, a people who will be His in the day when He makes up His jewels (Mal. 3:7), and it is a pity if we are not able to see what God so much admires.

If we are meek, we will more readily see the excellence of other people. There is a very beautiful passage in the second part of Bunyan's *The Pilgrim's Progress* that tells that, when Christiana and Mercy had both been bathed and clothed in fine linen, white and clean, they each began to think of the other as better than herself. If we also do this, we will not think as badly of this poor present life as some of us do now, but will go through it thanking God and praising His name, and so inheriting the earth.

With a gentle temper, a quiet spirit, and grace to keep you so, you will be inheriting the earth under any circumstances. If trouble should come, you will bow to it, as the willow bows to the wind and so escapes the injury that falls upon sturdier trees. If little vexations should come, you will not allow yourself to be vexed by them but will say, "With a little patience, they will all pass away."

I think I never admired Archbishop Leighton more than when I read about a certain incident in his life that had been recorded. He lived in a small house in Scotland and had only a manservant besides himself in the house. John, the manservant, was very forgetful; and, one morning, when he got up before his master, he thought he would like to have a day's fishing, so he went off and locked his master in. He fished until late in the evening, forgot all about his master, and when he came back, what do you think the bishop said to him? He simply said, "John, if you go out for a day's fishing another time, kindly leave me the key." He had had a happy day of prayer and study all by himself. If it had happened to us, we would have been fuming and fretting and getting up a nice lecture for John when he came back—and he richly deserved it—but I do not suppose it was worthwhile for the good man to worry himself about the situation. This incident is, I think, a good illustration of our text.

By Inheriting the Promised Land

But the text means more than I have yet said, for the promise, *"they shall inherit the earth,"* may be read, "they will inherit the land," that is, the Promised Land, the heavenly Canaan. These are the men who will inherit heaven; far up there they are all meek-spirited. There are no contentions there; pride cannot enter there. Anger, wrath, and malice never pollute the atmosphere of the celestial city. There, all bow before the King of Kings, and all rejoice in communion with Him and with one another. Beloved, if we are ever to enter heaven, we must fling away ambition and discontent and wrath and self-seeking and selfishness. May God's grace purge us of all these, for, as long as any of that evil leaven is in our soul, we cannot go where God is.

And then, dear friends, the text means even more than that—we will inherit this earth by and by. David wrote, *"The meek shall inherit the earth; and shall delight themselves in the abundance of peace"* (Ps. 37:11). After this earth has been purified by fire, after God has burned the works of men to ashes, and after every trace of corrupt humanity has been consumed by the fervent heat, then this earth will be fitted up again, angels will descend with new songs to sing, and the New Jerusalem will come down out of heaven from God in all her glory. And then upon this earth, where once was war, the trumpet will ring no more; there will be neither swords nor spears, and men will learn the arts of war no more (Mic. 4:3).

The meek will then possess the land, and every hill and valley will be glad, and every fruitful plain will ring with shouting of joy and peace and gladness throughout the long millennial day. May the Lord send it, and may we all be among the meek who will possess the new Eden, whose flowers will never wither, and where no serpent's trail will ever be seen!

But this must be the work of grace. We must be born again, or else our proud spirits will never be meek. And if we have been born again, let it be our joy, as long as we live, to show that we are the followers of the meek and lowly Jesus, with whose gracious words I close this chapter:

> Come unto me, all ye that labour and are heavy laden, and I will give you rest. Take my yoke upon you, and learn of me; for I am meek and lowly in heart: and ye shall find rest unto your souls. For my yoke is easy, and my burden is light. (Matt. 11:28–30)

So may it be, for Christ's sake! Amen.

4

Righteously Filled

*Blessed are they which do hunger and thirst after
righteousness: for they shall be filled.*
—Matthew 5:6

I previously remarked that each of the seven beatitudes rises above the one that precedes it, and
rises out of it. It is a higher thing to hunger and
thirst for righteousness than to be meek or to mourn
or to be poor in spirit. However, no man ever becomes hungry and thirsty for righteousness unless
he has first passed through the three preliminary
stages and has been convinced of his soul poverty,
has been made to mourn for sin, and has been rendered humble in the sight of God.

I have already shown that the meek man is one
who is contented with what God has given him in
this world, that he is one whose ambition is at an
end, and whose aspirations are not for things beneath the moon. Very well, then, having ceased to
hunger and thirst for this world, he is the man to
hunger and thirst for another and a better one.
Having said farewell to these material and perishing
things, he is the man to throw the whole intensity of
his nature into the pursuit of what is heavenly and
eternal, which is here described as *"righteousness."*

Man must first of all be cured of his ardor for earthly pursuits before he can feel fervor for heavenly ones. *"No man can serve two masters"* (Matt. 6:24), and until the old selfish principle has been driven out, and the man has become humble and meek, he will not begin to hunger and thirst for righteousness.

THE OBJECT THAT THE BLESSED MAN DESIRES

Proceeding at once to consider our text, we notice here what the blessed man desires as he hungers and thirsts for righteousness.

Righteousness before God

As soon as the Spirit of God quickens him and really makes him a blessed man, he begins to long for righteousness before God. He knows that he is a sinner and that, as a sinner, he is unrighteous and therefore is condemned at the bar of the Most High. But he wants to be righteous; he desires to have his iniquity removed and the defilement of the past blotted out. How can this be done? The question that he asks again and again is, "How can I be made righteous in the sight of God?" and he is never satisfied until he is told that Jesus Christ is made of God *"unto us wisdom, and righteousness, and sanctification, and redemption"* (1 Cor. 1:30). Then, when he sees that Christ died in the sinner's stead, he understands how the sinner's sins are put away. When he comprehends that Christ has worked out a perfect righteousness, not for Himself, but for the unrighteous, he comprehends how, by imputation, he is made righteous in the sight of God through the righteousness of Jesus Christ. But until he knows that, he hungers and thirsts for righteousness, and he is blessed in thus hungering and thirsting.

A Righteous Nature

After he has found Christ to be his righteousness as far as justification is concerned, this man then cries, "Alas! It is not enough for me to know that my sin is forgiven. I have a fountain of sin within my heart, and bitter waters continually flow from it. Oh, that my nature could be changed, so that I, the lover of sin, could be made a lover of what is good, so that I, now full of evil, could become full of holiness!" He begins to cry out for this, and he is blessed in the crying; but he never rests until the Spirit of God makes him a new creation in Christ Jesus (2 Cor. 5:17). Then he is renewed in the spirit of his mind, and God has given him, at least in measure, what he hungers and thirsts for, namely, righteousness of nature. He has passed from death unto life, from darkness to light. The things he formerly loved he now hates, and the things he then hated he now loves.

To Be Sanctified

After he is regenerated and justified, he still pants for righteousness in another sense. The new birth is the commencement of sanctification, and sanctification is the carrying on of the work commenced in regeneration; so the blessed man cries, "Lord, help me to be righteous in my character. You desire truth in the inward parts (Ps. 51:6); keep my whole nature pure. Let no temptation gain mastery over me. Subdue my pride; correct my judgment; keep my will in check; make me to be a holy man in the innermost temple of my being; and then let my conduct toward my fellowmen be in all respects all that it should be. Let me speak so that they can always believe my word. Let me act so that none can truly charge me with injustice. Let my life be a transparent one. Let it be, as far as it is possible, the life of Christ written over again." Thus, you see, the truly blessed man hungers and thirsts for justification, for regeneration, and for sanctification.

Perseverance in Grace

The blessed man thirsts to be kept right. If he has overcome one bad habit, he thirsts to put down all others. If he has acquired one virtue, he thirsts to acquire more. If God has given him much grace, he thirsts for more, and if he is in some respects like his Master, he perceives his defects and mourns over them and goes on to thirst to be still more like Jesus. He is always hungering and thirsting to be made right and to be kept right, so he prays for final perseverance and for perfection. He feels that he has such a hunger and thirst for righteousness that he will never be satisfied until he wakes up in the image of his Lord; that he will never be content until the last sin within him is subdued and he has no more tendency to do evil, but is out of the gunshot of temptation.

To See Righteousness Promoted

Such a man honestly wishes that others would do as they would be done by, and he tries, by his own example, to teach them to do so. He wishes that there were no fraud, no false witness, no perjury, no theft, no lasciviousness. He wishes that right ruled in the whole world. He would account it a happy day if every person could be blessed and if there were no need of punishment for offenses because they had ceased. He longs to hear that oppression has come to an end; he wants to see right government in every land. He longs for wars to cease. He longs that the rules and principles of right, and not force and the sharp edge of the sword, may govern all mankind. His daily prayer is, "Lord, let Your kingdom come, for Your kingdom is righteousness and peace."

When he sees any wrong done, he grieves over it. If he cannot alter it, he grieves all the more, and he labors as much as he is able to bear a protest against wrong of every sort. He hungers and thirsts for righteousness. He does not hunger and thirst that his own political party may get into power, but he does hunger and thirst that righteousness may be done in the land! He does not hunger and thirst that his own opinions may come to the forefront, and that his own sect or denomination may increase in numbers and influence, but he does desire that righteousness may come to the forefront. He does not crave for himself that he may be able to sway his fellowmen according to his own schemes, but he does wish that he could influence his fellowmen for that which is right and true, for his soul is all on fire with this one desire—righteousness—righteousness for himself, righteousness before God, righteousness between persons. This he longs to see, for this he hungers and thirsts, and in this Jesus says that he is blessed.

God Will Bless You

THE DESIRE ITSELF

It is said that he hungers and thirsts for right-eousness—a double description of his ardent desire for it. Surely it would have been enough for the man to hunger for it, but he thirsts as well; all the appetites, desires, and cravings of his spiritual nature go out toward what he wants above everything else, namely, righteousness. He feels that he has not attained it himself, and therefore he hungers and thirsts for it. He also laments that others have not attained it, and therefore he hungers and thirsts for them that they too may have it.

A Real Desire

Hunger and thirst are matters of fact, not fancy. Suppose that you meet a man who tells you that he is so hungry that he is almost starving, and you say to him, "Nonsense, my dear fellow, just forget all about it. It is a mere whim of yours, for you can live very well without food if you like." Why, he knows that you are mocking him. And if you could surprise some poor wretch who had been floating away in a boat cast away at sea and had not been able for days to moisten his mouth except with the briny water that had only increased his thirst, and if you were to say to him, "Thirst! It is only your imagination. You are nervous, that is all; you need no drink." In response, the man would soon tell you that he knows better than that, for he must drink or die.

There is nothing in the world that is more real than hunger and thirst, and the truly blessed man has such a real passion, desire, and craving for

68

righteousness that it can only be likened to hunger and thirst. He must have his sins pardoned; he must be clothed in the righteousness of Christ; he must be sanctified; and he feels that it will break his heart if he cannot get rid of sin. He pines, he longs, he prays to be made holy; he cannot be satisfied without this righteousness, and his hungering and thirsting for it are very real.

A Most Natural Desire

And not only is it real, it is natural for men who need bread to hunger; you do not have to tell them when to hunger or when to thirst. If they do not have bread and water, they hunger and thirst naturally. So, when the Spirit of God has changed a person's nature, that new nature hungers and thirsts for righteousness. The old nature never did, never could, and never would do so. It hungers after the husks that the swine eat, but the new nature hungers for righteousness; it must do so, for it cannot help itself. You do not need to say to the quickened man, "Desire holiness." Why, he would gives his eyes to possess it. You do not need to say to a man who is under conviction of sin, "Desire the righteousness of Christ." He would be willing to lay down his life if he could only obtain it. He hungers and thirsts for righteousness from the absolute necessity of his nature.

An Intense Desire

What is more intense than hunger? When a man cannot find any nourishment, his hunger seems to eat him up; his yearnings after bread are terrible. I have heard it said that in the Bread Riots, the cry of the men and women for bread was far more terrible to hear than the cry of "Fire!" when some great city has been burning. "Bread! Bread!" He who does not have it feels that he must have it.

The cravings of thirst are even more intense. It is said that you may alleviate the pangs of hunger, but thirst makes life itself a burden; a man must drink or die. Well now, such is the intense longing for righteousness of a man whom God has blessed. He wants it so urgently that he says, in the anguish of his heart, that he cannot live without it. The psalmist said, *"My soul waiteth for the Lord more than they that watch for the morning: I say, more than they that watch for the morning"* (Ps. 130:6).

A Very Painful Desire

There is no other desire that is quite like the desire of a quickened man for righteousness; therefore, it can become quite painful. Hunger and thirst, endured up to a certain point, involve the very keenest of pangs, and a man who is seeking the righteousness of Christ is full of unutterable woe until he finds it. The Christian who is warring against his corruptions is led to cry, *"O wretched man that I am!"* (Rom. 7:24), until he learns that Christ has won the victory for him. The servant of Christ who desires to reclaim the nations and to bring his fellowmen to follow what is right and good is often the subject of unutterable pangs. He bears the burden of the Lord and goes about his work like a man who has too heavy a burden to carry. It is painful indeed

70

to the soul to be made to hunger and thirst for righteousness.

A Most Energetic Desire

The expressions in our text also indicate that
this is a most energetic desire. A man who is hungry
will be driven to do almost anything. We have an old
proverb that "hunger breaks through stone walls,"
and, certainly, a man who is hungry and thirsty for
righteousness will break through anything to get it.
Have we not known the sincere penitent to travel
many miles in order to get where he could hear the
Gospel? Has he not often lost his night's rest and
brought himself almost to death's door by his persis-
tence in pleading with God for pardon? And as to the
man who is saved and who desires to see others
saved, how often, in his desire to lead them in the
right way, will he surrender home comforts to go to
a distant land; how often will he bring upon himself
the scorn and contempt of the ungodly because zeal
for righteousness works mightily within his spirit!

I would like to see many of these hungry and
thirsty ones as members of our churches, preaching
in our pulpits, toiling in our Sunday schools and
mission stations, men and women who feel that they
must see Christ's kingdom come, or else they will
hardly be able to live. This holy craving for righteousness, which the Holy Spirit implants in a Christian's soul, becomes imperious; it is not merely
energetic, but it dominates his entire being. For this
he puts aside all other wishes and desires. He can be
a failure, but he must be righteous. He can be ridiculed, but he must hold fast to his integrity. He can

endure scorn, but he must declare the truth. *"Righteousness"* he must have; his spirit demands it by an appetite that lords it over all other pains and propensities, and truly *"blessed"* is the man in whom this is the case.

A Sign of Spiritual Life

Nobody who was spiritually dead ever hungered for righteousness. In all the catacombs there has never yet been found a dead man hungering or thirsting, and there never will be. If you hunger and thirst for righteousness, you are spiritually alive. And it is also a proof of spiritual health. Physicians will tell you that they regard a good appetite as being one of the signs that a man's body is in a healthy state, and it is the same with the soul.

Oh, to have a ravenous appetite for Christ! Oh, to be greedy for the best things! Oh, to be covetous for holiness, in fact, to hunger and thirst after everything that is right and good and pure and lovely and of good repute. May the Lord send us more of this intense hunger and thirst!

It is the very opposite condition of that of the self-satisfied and the self-righteous. Pharisees never hunger and thirst for righteousness; they have all the righteousness they want, and they even think that they have some to spare for that poor publican over there who cries, *"God be merciful to me a sinner"* (Luke 18:13). If a man thinks that he is perfect, what can he know about hungering and thirsting? He is filled already with all that he wants, and he also thinks that he could give of his redundant riches to his poor brother who is sighing over his imperfections. For my part, I am quite content to have the blessing of hungering and thirsting still, for that blessing stands side by side with another experience, namely, that of being filled. When one is in one sense filled, yet in another sense hungers still for more, this makes up the complete beatitude, *"Blessed are they which do hunger and thirst after righteousness: for they shall be filled."*

THE BLESSING ITSELF

The blessing is the benediction that Christ pronounces over those who hunger and thirst for righteousness: *"They shall be filled."*

A Unique Blessing

No one else ever gets *"filled."* A man desires meat; he eats it, and is filled for a little while; but he is soon hungry again. A man desires drink, and he has it, but is soon thirsty again. But a man who hungers and thirsts for righteousness will be so *"filled"* that he will never again thirst as he thirsted before.

Many hunger and thirst after gold, but nobody ever yet filled his soul with gold; it cannot be done. The richest man who ever lived was never quite as rich as he would have liked to be. Men have tried to fill their souls with worldly possessions; they have added field to field, and farm to farm, and street to street, and town to town, until it seemed as if they would be left alone in the land; but no man ever yet could fill his soul with an estate, however vast it might be. A few more acres were wanted to square off that corner, or to join that farm to the main body of his territory, or if he could only have had a little more upland, he might have been satisfied; but he did not get it, so he was still discontented. Alexander conquered the world, but it could not fill his soul; he wanted more worlds to conquer. And if you and I could own a dozen worlds, were we possessors of all the stars, and if we could call all space our own, we would not find enough to fill our immortal spirits; we would only be magnificently poor, a couple of imperial paupers.

God has so made man's heart that nothing can ever fill it but God Himself. There is such a hunger and thirst put into the quickened man that he discerns his necessity, and he knows that only Christ can supply that necessity. When a man is saved, he has obtained all that he wants. When he gets Christ, he is satisfied.

I remember a foolish woman asking me, some years ago, to let her tell my fortune. I said to her, "I can tell you yours, but I don't want to know mine; mine is already made, for I have everything that I want."

"But," she said, "can't I promise you something for years to come?"

"No," I answered, "I don't want anything; I have everything that I want. I am perfectly satisfied and perfectly contented."

And I can say the same now; I do not know anything that anybody could offer to me that would increase my satisfaction. If God will but bless the souls of men, and save them, and get glory to Himself, I am filled with contentment; I want nothing more. I do not believe that any man can honestly say as much as that unless he has found Christ, but if he has by faith laid hold upon the Savior, then he has grasped what always brings the blessing with it. He *"shall be filled."* It is a unique blessing.

An Appropriate Blessing

A man is hungry and thirsty; how can you take away his hunger without filling him with food, and how can you remove his thirst without filling him with drink, at least in sufficient quantity to satisfy him? So Christ's promise concerning the people who hunger and thirst for righteousness is, *"They shall be filled."* He wants righteousness; he will have righteousness. He wants God; he will have God. He wants a new heart; he will have a new heart. He wants to be kept from sin; he will be kept from sin. He wants to be made perfect; he will be made perfect. He wants to live where there are none who sin; he will be taken away to dwell where there will be no sinners forever and ever.

A Large and Abundant Blessing

In addition to being unique and appropriate, this blessing is very large and abundant. Christ said, *"Blessed are they which do hunger and thirst after righteousness: for they shall"*—have a meal by the way? Oh, no! *"For they shall"*—have a little comfort every now and then? Oh, no! *"For they shall be filled."* The Greek word might even be better rendered, "they shall lie satiated." They will have all they need, enough and to spare. They who hunger and thirst for righteousness will be filled—filled to the brim. How true this is!

Here is a man who says, "I am condemned in the sight of God; I feel and know that no actions of mine can ever make me righteous before Him. I have given up all hope of self-justification." Listen! Will you believe in Jesus Christ, the Son of God, and take Him to stand before God as your Substitute and Representative? "I will. I do trust in Him, and in Him alone." Well then, know that you have received from Christ a righteousness that may well satisfy you! All that God could rightly ask of you was the perfect righteousness of a man; for, being a man, that is all the righteousness that you could be expected to present to God. But, in the righteousness of Christ, you have the perfect righteousness of a man, and more than that; you also have the righteousness of God. Think of that! Father Adam, in his perfection, wore the righteousness of man, and it was lovely to look upon as long as it lasted, but if you trust in Jesus, you are wearing the righteousness of God, for Christ was God as well as man.

Now, when a man attains to that experience and knows that, having believed in Jesus, God looks upon him as if the righteousness of Jesus were his own righteousness, and in fact attributes to him the divine righteousness that is Christ's, that man is filled. He is more than filled; he is satiated. All that his soul could possibly desire he already possesses in Christ Jesus.

I told you that the man also wanted a new nature. He said, "O God, I long to get rid of these evil propensities. I want to have this defiled body of mine made to be a proper temple for You. I want to be made like my Lord and Savior, so that I may be able to walk with Him in heaven forever and ever." Listen!

If you believe in Jesus Christ, this is what has been done to you: you have received into your nature, by the Word of God, an incorruptible seed, *"which liveth and abideth for ever"* (1 Pet. 1:23). That is already in you if you are a believer in Jesus, and it can no more die than God Himself can die, for it is a divine nature.

"The grass withereth, and the flower thereof falleth away: but the word of the Lord"—that Word that you have received if you have believed in Jesus—*"endureth for ever"* (1 Pet. 1:24–25). The water that Christ has given you will be a well of water in you springing up into everlasting life (John 4:14). In the moment of our regeneration, a new nature is imparted to us, of which the apostle Peter said,

> *The God and Father of our Lord Jesus Christ... according to his abundant mercy hath begotten us again unto a lively hope by the resurrection of Jesus Christ from the dead, to an inheritance incorruptible, and undefiled, and that fadeth not away.*   *(1 Pet. 1:3–4)*

The same apostle also stated that believers are *"partakers of the divine nature, having escaped the corruption that is in the world through lust"* (2 Pet. 1:4). Is not that a blessed beginning for those who hunger and thirst for righteousness?

But, listen further: God the Holy Spirit, the third Person of the blessed Trinity, condescends to come and dwell in all believers. Paul wrote to the church of God at Corinth, *"Know ye not that your body is the temple of the Holy Ghost?"* (1 Cor. 6:19). God dwells in you, my brother or sister in Christ.

Does this truth not astonish you? Sin dwells in you, but the Holy Spirit has also come to dwell in you and to drive sin out of you.

The Devil assails you and tries to capture your spirit and to make it like those in his own infernal den, but the Eternal has himself come down and enshrined Himself within you. The Holy Spirit is dwelling within your heart if you are a believer in Jesus; Christ Himself is *"in you, the hope of glory"* (Col. 1:27). If you really want righteousness, dear soul, surely you have it here: the nature changed and made like the nature of God; the ruling principle altered; sin dethroned; and the Father, the Son, and the Holy Spirit dwelling within you as your Lord and Master. Why, I think that, however much you may hunger and thirst for righteousness, you must count yourself well filled, since you have these immeasurable blessings.

Listen yet again, my brother or sister in Christ. You will be kept and preserved even to the end. He who has begun to cleanse you will never stop the work until He has made you without spot or wrinkle or any such thing. He never begins a work that He cannot or will not complete. He has never failed in anything that He has undertaken, and He never will fail.

Your corruptions have their heads already broken, and though your sins still rebel, it is but a struggling gasp for life. The weapons of victorious grace will slay them all and end the strife forever. The sins that trouble you today will be like those Egyptians who pursued the children of Israel into the Red Sea; you will see them no more forever. *"The God of peace shall bruise Satan under your feet shortly"* (Rom. 16:20). As surely as you have believed in Christ, poor imperfect worm of the dust as you are, you will walk with Him, clothed in white, on golden streets, in that city within whose gates there will never enter anything that defiles, *"but* [instead] *they which are written in the Lamb's book of life"* (Rev. 21:27).

Yes, believer, you will be near and like your God. Do you hear this? You who hunger and thirst for righteousness will have it without limit, for you will be one of the *"partakers of the inheritance of the saints in light"* (Col. 1:12). You will be able to gaze upon God in His ineffable glory and to dwell with the devouring fire and the everlasting burning of His unsullied purity. You will be able to see the God who is a consuming fire, and yet not be afraid, for there will be nothing in you to be consumed. You will be spotless, innocent, pure, immortal as your God Himself. Will this not satisfy you?

"Ah," you say, "it satisfies me for myself; but I would gladly like to see my children righteous, too." Then commend them to that God who loves their father and their mother, and ask Him to bless your children as He blessed Isaac for Abraham's sake, and blessed Jacob for Isaac's sake. "Oh," you say, "but I also want to see my neighbors saved." Then hunger for their souls, thirst for their souls as you have hungered and thirsted for your own, and God will teach you how to talk to them. Probably then, as you are hungering and thirsting for their souls, He will make you the means of their conversion.

There is also this truth to solace you: there will be righteousness all over this world one day. Millions still reject Christ, but He has a people who will not reject Him. The masses of mankind at present flee from Him, but *"the Lord knoweth them that are his"* (2 Tim. 2:19). As many as the Father gave to Christ will surely come to Him. Christ will not be disappointed; His cross will not have been set up in vain. *"He shall see his seed, he shall prolong his days, and the pleasure of the LORD shall prosper in his hand. He shall see of the travail of his soul, and shall be satisfied"* (Isa. 53:10–11).

Well may you groan because of the idols that do not fall and the oppressions that do not come to an end and the wailing of the widows and the weeping of the orphans and the sighing of those who sit in darkness and see no light, but there will be an end of all this. Brighter days than these are coming; either the Gospel will cover the earth, or else Christ Himself will personally come. Whichever it is, it is not for me to decide, but, somehow or other, the day will come when God will reign without a rival over all the earth; be sure of that. The hour will come when the great multitude, *"as the voice of many waters, and as the voice of mighty thunderings,"* will say, *"Alleluia: for the Lord God omnipotent reigneth"* (Rev. 19:6).

If we are hungering and thirsting for righteousness, we are on the winning side. The battle may go against us just now. Evils that our forefathers routed may come back with superior strength and cunning, and for a little while the courage of the saints may be damped, and their armies may waver. But the Lord still lives, and as the Lord lives, righteousness alone will triumph, and all iniquity and every false way must be trampled underfoot. Fight on, for you must ultimately be victors. You cannot be beaten unless the Eternal Himself could be overthrown, and that can never be.

Blessed is the man who knows that the cause that he has championed is a righteous one, for he may know that in the final chapter of the world's history, its triumph must be recorded. He may be dead and gone; he may only sow the seed, but his sons will reap the harvest. Men will speak of him with grave respect as of a man who lived before his time and who deserves honor from those who follow him. Stand up for the right! Hold fast to your principles, my brothers and sisters in Christ! Follow after holiness and righteousness in every shape and form. Let no one bribe you or turn you away from this blessed Book and its immortal tenets. Follow after what is true, not what is patronized by the great; what is just, not what sits in the seat of human authority; and follow after this with a hunger and a thirst that are insatiable, and you will yet be *"filled."*

Do you want to be up there in the day when the Prince of Truth and Right will review His armies? Do you want to be up there when the jubilant shout will split the heavens, "The King of Kings and Lord of Lords has conquered all His foes, and the Devil and all his hosts are put to flight"? Do you want to be up there, I say, when all His trophies of victory are displayed and the Lamb that was slain will be the reigning Monarch of all the nations, gathering sheaves of scepters beneath His arms and treading on the crowns of princes as worn out and worthless? Do you want to be there then? Then be here now— here where the fight rages, here where the King's standard is unfurled—and say to your God, "O Lord,

since I have found righteousness in Christ, and I am
myself saved, I am pledged to stand for the right and
for the truth as long as I live; so keep me faithful
even unto death."

As I close this chapter, I pronounce over all of
you who are trusting in Jesus, the fourth benediction spoken by Christ on the Mount of Beatitude:
*"Blessed are they which do hunger and thirst after
righteousness: for they shall be filled."* Amen.

5

The Hunger and Thirst That Are Blessed

Blessed are they which do hunger and thirst after righteousness: for they shall be filled.
—Matthew 5:6

Because man had perfect righteousness before the Fall, he enjoyed perfect blessedness. If you and I will, by divine grace, attain to blessedness hereafter, it will be because God has restored us to righteousness. As it was in the first Paradise, so must it be in the second: righteousness is essential to the blessedness of man. We cannot be truly happy and live in sin. Holiness is the natural element of blessedness, and it can no more live out of that element than a fish could live in the fire. The happiness of man must come through his righteousness: his being right with God, with man, with himself—indeed, his being right all around.

Then, since the first blessedness of our unfallen state is gone, and the blessedness of perfection hereafter is not yet come, how can we be blessed in the interval that lies between? The answer is, *"Blessed are they which do hunger and thirst after righteousness."* Though they have not yet attained the righteousness

they desire, even the longing for it makes them a
blessed people. The massive blessedness of the past
and the priceless blessedness of the eternal future
are joined together by a band of present blessedness.
The band is not as massive as those two things that
it unites, but it is of the same metal, has been fash-
ioned by the same hand, and is as indestructible as
the treasures that it binds together.

I am going to continue my discussion of this
hunger and thirst from the last chapter. I feel so un-
fit for the effort that I must correct myself and say
that I hunger and thirst to expound on this, but that
is all the power I have. Oh, that I, too, may be filled
for your sakes! May the Spirit of the Lord fulfill my
intense desire to minister to you from this beatitude
of our Lord Jesus, *"Blessed are they which do hunger
and thirst after righteousness: for they shall be
filled."*

First, then, in our text we have mention of sin-
gular appetites—*"hunger and thirst,"* not for bread
and water, but, *"after righteousness."* Secondly, we
have a remarkable declaration about these hungering
people—Jesus stated that they are *"blessed,"* or
happy, and beyond a doubt His judgment is true.
Thirdly, a special satisfaction meeting their necessity
is mentioned in our text, and in its foresight, it makes
them blessed: our Savior said, *"They shall be filled."*

SINGULAR APPETITES

Different Forms

They hunger and they thirst; the two most ur-
gent needs of the body are used to set forth the

cravings of the soul for righteousness. Hunger and thirst are different, but they are both the language of keen desire. He who has ever felt either of these two knows how sharp are the pangs they bring, and if the two are combined in one craving, they make up a restless, terrible, unconquerable passion. Who will resist a man hungering and thirsting? His whole being fights to satisfy his awful needs. Blessed are they who have a longing for righteousness, which no one word can fully describe and no one craving can set forth. Hunger must be joined with thirst, to set forth the strength and eagerness of the desire for righteousness.

This desire is like hunger and thirst in constancy; not that it is always equally raging, for the hungry man is not always equally in pain, but still, he can never quite forget the gnawing within, the burning at the heart. Blessed is the man who is always desiring righteousness with an insatiable longing that nothing can turn aside. Hunger and thirst are irrepressible. Until you feed a man, his wants will continue to devour him. You may give a hungry man the best music that was ever drawn from strings or breathed from pipes, but his cravings are not soothed; you do but mock him. You may set before him the fairest prospect, but unless in that prospect a loaf of bread and a cup of water stands conspicuous, he has no heart for flood or field, mountain or forest.

They are blessed, says Christ, who, with regard to righteousness, are always seeking it and cannot be satisfied until they find it. The desire for righteousness, which a man must have in order to be blessed, is not a faint one, in which he feebly says, "I wish I could be righteous." It is also not a passing outburst of good desires.

It is a longing that, like hunger and thirst, abides with a man and masters him. He carries it to his work, carries it to his house, carries it to his bed, carries it wherever he himself goes, for it rules him with its imperative demands. As the horse leech cries, *"Give, give"* (Prov. 30:15), so the heart cries after purity, integrity, and holiness when once it has learned to hunger and thirst for righteousness.

Concentrated upon One Object

The man hungers and thirsts for righteousness and nothing else. For the most part, theological works say either that this is imputed righteousness or implanted righteousness. No doubt these things are meant, but I do not care to insert an adjective where there is none; the text does not say either "imputed" or "implanted"—why do we need to mend it? It is righteousness that a man pants for—righteousness in all its meanings.

First, he feels that he is not right with God, and the discovery causes him great distress. The Spirit of God shows him that he is all wrong with God, for he has broken the law that he ought to have kept, and he has not paid the homage and love that were justly due. The same Spirit makes him long to get right with God, and his conscience being stirred up, he cannot rest until this is done. This, of course, includes the pardon of his offenses, and the giving to him of a righteousness that will make him acceptable to God. He eagerly cries to God for this blessing. One of the bitterest pangs of his soul hunger is the dread that this need can never be met. How can man be just with God? It is the unique glory of the Gospel that it reveals the righteousness of God—the method by which sinners can be put right with God—and this comes with unique sweetness to one who is striving and praying, and hungering and thirsting for righteousness. When he hears of righteousness by faith in the Lord Jesus Christ, he leaps at it and lays hold upon it, for it exactly meets his case.

The hunger now takes another form. The pardoned and justified man now desires to be right in his conduct and language and thought; he pines to be righteous in his whole life. He wants to be marked by integrity, kindness, mercifulness, love, and everything else that makes up a right condition of things toward his fellow creatures. He ardently desires to be correct in his feelings and conduct toward God; he craves to know, obey, pray, praise, and love his God. He cannot rest until he stands toward God and man as he ought to stand. His longing is not only to be treated as righteous by God, which comes through the atoning blood and righteousness of the Lord Jesus Christ, but that he may be actually righteous before the heart-searching God. And this will not be sufficient for him; not only must his conduct be right, but he pants to be right himself.

He finds within himself ungodly desires, and he wants these to be utterly destroyed. He finds tendencies toward unrighteousness, and although he resists these and overcomes them, the tendencies themselves are abhorrent to him. He finds longings after pleasures that are forbidden, and though he rejects those pleasures with loathing, his trouble is that he should have any inclination toward them. He wants to be so renewed so that sin will have no power over him. He has learned that a lustful look is adultery, that a covetous desire is theft, and that wrongful anger is murder; therefore, he craves not only to be free from the look and the desire and the passion, but even from the tendency in that direction. He longs to have the fountain of his being cleansed. Ho hungers to *"put on the new man, which after God is created in righteousness and true holiness"* (Eph. 4:24). He thirsts to be *"renewed in knowledge after the image of him that created him"* (Col. 3:10). He cannot be content until he is himself like Jesus, who is the image of the invisible God, the mirror of righteousness and peace.

But, mind you, if the man should attain to this, his hunger and thirst would only take another direction. The godly man hungers and thirsts to see righteousness in others. At times, when he sees the conduct of those around him, he cries, *"My soul is among lions: and I lie even among them that are set on fire"* (Ps. 57:4). The more holy he becomes, the more sin vexes his righteous soul, and he cries, *"Woe is me, that I sojourn in Mesech, that I dwell in the tents of Kedar!"* (Ps. 120:5). He often wishes that he had *"wings like a dove,"* that he might *"fly away, and be at rest"* (Ps. 55:6). Like Cowper, he cries,

> Oh, for a lodge in some vast wilderness,
> Some boundless contiguity of shade,
> Where rumour of oppression and deceit,

The Hunger and Thirst That Are Blessed

> Of unsuccessful or successful war,
> Might never reach me more!

He hungers for godly company; he thirsts to see the unholy made holy; and therefore he cries in his daily prayer, *"Thy kingdom come. Thy will be done in earth, as it is in heaven"* (Matt. 6:10). With hunger and thirst he cries, "Lord, end the reign of sin! Lord, cast down idols! Lord, chase error from the earth! Lord, turn men from lust and greed and cruelty and drunkenness." He wants to live for righteousness and die for righteousness; the zeal of it consumes him.

Believers, I hope you have been able to follow, by your own knowledge, the various movements of this absorbing passion for righteousness that I have thus feebly sketched for you.

Very Discriminating

Note well that these concentrated appetites are very discriminating. The man does not long for twenty things, but only for one thing, and for that one thing by itself. The hunger and the thirst are *"after righteousness."* The man does not hunger for wealth; he would rather be poor and righteous than be rich and evil. He does not hunger for health, though he would wish to have that great blessing; he would rather be sick and have righteousness than enjoy good health and be unrighteous. He does not even set before himself the rewards of righteousness as his great object. These are very desirable—the respect of one's peers, peace of mind, and communion with God are by no means little things—but he does not make these the chief objects of his desire, for he knows that they will be added to him in the first place if he seeks for righteousness itself.

If there were no heaven, the godly man would wish to be righteous; if there were no hell, he would dread unrighteousness. His hunger and thirst are for honesty, purity, rectitude, and holiness; he hungers and he thirsts to be what God would have him to be.

Always distinguish between seeking heaven and seeking God, between shunning hell and shunning sin, for any hypocrite will desire heaven and dread hell, but only the sincere hunger for righteousness. The thief would shun the prison, but he would like to be once more at his theft; the murderer would want to escape the gallows, but he would readily enough have his hand on his dagger again. The desire to be happy, the wish to be at ease in conscience—these are poor things. The true and noble hunger of the soul is the desire to be right for the sake of righteousness. Oh, to be holy, whether that should mean joy or sorrow! Oh, to be pure in heart, whether that would bring me honor or contempt! This is the blessed thirst.

Working in Their Own Way

Hunger and thirst are not the bed makers of the house of humanity. No, they ring the alarm bells and even shake the foundations of the house. The starving man cannot sustain himself. Ultimately, his terrible needs may reduce him to a passive condition by way of faintness and insensibility, but while sense remains in the man, hunger and thirst are fierce forces that nerve him to the most intense endeavors.

The Hunger and Thirst That Are Blessed

When a prisoner was set at the prison gate to plead for the poor debtors in the old times, he did plead. Reduced to a skeleton, he rattled the box in the ears of persons passing by and cried most piteously so that they would give something to the poor debtors who were starving inside. How a hungry man looks at you! His very look is a piercing prayer. A man who hungers and thirsts for righteousness pleads with God with his whole soul. Prayer is no counterfeit with him.

The man who is hungry and thirsty for righteousness is the wrestling man. This makes him also the active man, for hunger will break through stone walls; he will do anything for food. The worst of it is that he often attempts foolish things; he tries to stay his hunger with what is not bread and spends his labor on what does not satisfy. Still, this only proves how energetic these appetites are, and how they call out every power of humanity when they are set upon righteousness.

An Uncommon Hunger and Thirst

Beloved, multitudes of people in the world never hunger and thirst for righteousness. Some of you would like to be saved, but you can do very well if you are not. A man who is hungry and thirsty will never say, "I would like a meal, but I can do very well without it," and you do not hunger and thirst if you can rest without the blessing you profess to value. If you hunger and thirst for righteousness, you want it at once. These cravings will not tolerate delay; they clamor for immediate supplies. The hungry man's tense is the present.

God Will Bless You

Oh, how many there are who, by their delay and by their carelessness, prove that they never hunger and thirst for righteousness! I also see others who are righteous already. They are as good as they want to be. Hear someone say, "I do not make any profession of religion, but I am a great deal better than many who do." Oh, yes, I know you, and the Virgin Mary knew you, for she said in her song, *"He hath filled the hungry with good things; and the rich he hath sent empty away"* (Luke 1:53). You will one day be emptied, but you will never be filled. Why should you be? You are so blown up with wind that there is no room for the heavenly substance within your heart.

Many refuse the Lord Jesus Christ, who is the bread of heaven. No man can be said to be hungry if he refuses wholesome food. When your child sits down to eat and says that he does not want any dinner, he is evidently not hungry. Those who put Christ away and will have nothing to do with His atonement and His sanctification are not hungry for righteousness.

Many criticize the little things of the Gospel, the insignificant matters of the minister's voice, tone, and appearance. When a man sits down to dinner and begins to notice that one of the dishes is chipped, and one of the roses in the center has an insect on it, and the saltshaker is not in the right position, and the parsley is not nicely arranged around the cold meat, that fellow is not hungry. Feed a poor dockyard laborer, or, better still, his wife and children, and they will eat meat without mustard, and bread without butter. The hungry man will eat fat as well as lean, I guarantee. Preaching would not so often be submitted to silly remarks if men were really hungry after the truth. "Give me a knife and a chance," says the man who is hungry. "Give me the Gospel," says the anxious inquirer, "and I care nothing for the eloquence." Beloved, I wish you may so hunger and thirst for righteousness that trifles may be trifles to you, and the essential truth be your only concern.

Alas, there are some who we are sure do not hunger and thirst for righteousness, for they do not care even to hear about it. When your child stays out in the yard at dinnertime, you may be sure that he or she is not very hungry. The dinner bell is a very prevailing reasoner when it finds its arguments within the listener. As soon as there is notification that food is to be had, the hungry man hastens to the table. I strongly desire that we had more spiritually hungry people to tell about God. He who preached to the spiritually hungry would be a blessed preacher, for he would be preaching to a blessed people. *"Blessed are they which do hunger and thirst after righteousness: for they shall be filled."*

THE REMARKABLE DECLARATION OF OUR LORD

Christ said, *"Blessed are they which do hunger and thirst after righteousness."* This is a paradox. It does not seem possible that people could be hungry and thirsty, and yet be blessed. Hunger and thirst bring pain. I know you, my friend; you are saying to yourself, "Oh, that I could be right! I am a great sinner; oh, that I were forgiven! Oh, that I could become righteous before God!" Another is saying,

"I trust I am forgiven and saved, but I feel a dreadful fear that I will fall into sin. *'O wretched man that I am'* (Rom. 7:24), to have sinful tendencies! Oh, that I could be perfect and altogether delivered from this embodied death that surrounds me in the form of a sinful nature!" Or, perhaps, another friend is crying, "God has been very gracious to me; but my children, my husband, my brother, are living in sin, and these are my daily burden. I have a very heavy heart because they do not know the Lord." Listen, dear friend, and be encouraged; whatever form your hunger for righteousness may take, you are a blessed person. Although you endure that pain about yourself and others, you are blessed.

Hunger and thirst often cause a sinking feeling, and that sinking feeling sometimes turns to a deadly faintness. It may be I am speaking to one who has reached that stage; to him I say, "You are blessed." I hear you sighing, "Oh, that I could be what I want to be! *'O wretched man that I am! who shall deliver me from the body of this death?'* (Rom. 7:24). These inward corruptions, these evil imaginations, they will kill me; I cannot bear them. God has taught me to love what is good, and now *'to will is present with me; but how to perform that which is good I find not'* (Rom. 7:18). Even my prayers are interrupted by wandering thoughts, and my tears of repentance have sin mixed with them." Beloved, I understand that faintness and sinking, that groaning and pining; but, nevertheless, you are blessed, for the text says, and it is a very remarkable saying, *"Blessed are they which do hunger and thirst after righteousness."*

The Hunger and Thirst That Are Blessed

WHY ARE SUCH PEOPLE BLESSED?

Jesus Said They Are

If Christ said that the hungry and thirsty are blessed, we do not need any further proof. If, looking around the crowd, our Lord passed by those who were self-satisfied; and if His eyes focused on the men who were sighing and crying and hungering and thirsting for righteousness; and if, with a smiling face, He said, "These are the blessed ones"; then depend upon it, they are indeed so. For, I know that those whom He declares to be blessed must be blessed indeed. I would rather be one whom Christ counted blessed than one who was so esteemed by all the world, for the Lord Jesus knows better than men do.

They Have Been Made to Know Right Values

The man hungering for righteousness ought to consider himself a happy man, because he now knows the right value of things. Before, he set a high value upon worthless pleasure, and he reckoned the dross of the praise of men to be as pure gold. Now, he values righteousness and is not like the child who prizes glass beads more than pearls. He has already obtained some measure of righteousness, for his judgment reckons rightly. He ought to be thankful for being so far enlightened. Once he put bitter for sweet, and sweet for bitter; darkness for light, and light for darkness; but now the Lord has brought him to know what is good and what it is that the

Lord requires of him. In gaining this right judgment, he is a blessed man and is on the way to still greater blessedness.

They Have a Heart for What Is Good

Once such a man only cared for earthly comforts; now he hungers and thirsts for righteousness. "Give me a bit of meat in the pot," cries the worldling, "and I will leave your precious righteousness to those who want it," but this man prizes the spiritual above the natural. Righteousness is happiness to him. His one cry is, "Give me righteousness." His whole heart is set on it, and this is no common privilege. He who is filled with the desire of what God approves is himself approved. To such a man is given a magnanimity that is of more than royal nature, and for it he should be grateful to God.

Many More Common Hungers Die Out

One master passion, like Aaron's rod, swallows up all the rest. He hungers and thirsts for righteousness; therefore, he is done with the craving of lust, the greed of avarice, the passion of hate, and the pining of ambition. I have known sickly men to be overtaken by a disease that has driven out their old complaints; a fresh fire has put out the former ones. So men, under the influence of a craving for righteousness, have found land hunger and gold hunger and pride thirst and lust thirst to come to an end. The new affections have expelled the old, even as the Israelites drove the Canaanites into the mountains, or slew them. God alone can give this hungering and thirsting for righteousness, and one of its grand qualities is that it drives out the groveling and sinful lusting that otherwise would consume our hearts.

They Have Been Delivered from Many Delusions

The most common delusion is that man can get everything that he needs in religion from himself. Most men are deluded in this way; they think they have a springing well of power within, from which they can cleanse, revive, and satisfy themselves. Try this doctrine with a hungry man or a thirsty man: "My dear fellow, you need not be hungry—you can satisfy yourself from yourself."

What is his answer? "I have tied a hunger belt around myself to keep down the hunger, but I did not find even that within myself. I am hungry and must have food from outside, or I will die." He cannot eat his own heart or feed upon his own liver; it is not possible for him to satisfy his hunger from himself.

The common spiritual delusion of men is of the same kind. They imagine that they can, by an effort of their own, satisfy their consciences, make themselves pure, and produce righteousness of character. Still they dream of bringing a clean thing out of something unclean.

Let spiritual hunger and thirst come upon them, and let them escape from this snare. The spiritually hungry man cries, "Self-trust is a refuge of lies. I must be helped from above. I must be saved by grace, or I will remain unrighteous to the end." Spiritual hunger and thirst are wonderful teachers of the doctrines of grace and very speedy dispellers of the illusions of pride.

They Are Already Worked upon by the Holy Spirit

Hunger and thirst for righteousness are always the production of the Holy Spirit. It is not natural for man to love the good and the holy. He loves what is wrong and evil; he loves the trespass or the omission; but he does not seek after strict rectitude before God. But when a man is hungry to be true, hungry to be sober, hungry to be pure, hungry to be holy, his hunger is a blessing from heaven and a promise of the heaven from which it came.

They Are in Accord with the Lord Jesus Christ

When our Lord was here, He hungered for righteousness, longing to do and to be in accordance with His Father's will. His disciples, on one occasion, went away to the city to buy meat, and He, being left alone, thirsted to bless the poor sinful woman of Samaria, who came to the well to draw water. He said to her, *"Give me to drink"* (John 4:7), not only to commence the conversation, but because He thirsted to make that woman righteous. He thirsted to convince her of her sin and lead her to saving faith, and when He had done so, His desire was gratified. When His disciples came back, though He had not touched a morsel of bread or a drop of water, He said, *"I have meat to eat that ye know not of....My*

*meat is to do the will of him that sent me, and to fin-
ish his work"* (vv. 32, 34).

Our Lord, on the cross, said, *"I thirst"* (John
19:28), and that thirst of His lip and of His mouth
was but the index of the deeper thirst of His heart
and soul that righteousness might reign by His
death. He died so that the righteousness of God
might be vindicated; He lives so that the righteousness of God may be proclaimed; He pleads so that
the righteousness of God may be brought home to
sinners; He reigns so that this righteousness may
chase out of this world the iniquity that now destroys it.

When you hunger and thirst for righteousness
in any one of the ways I have described, you are in a
measure a partaker with Christ and have fellowship
with Him in His heart's desire. As He is blessed, so
are you, for *"Blessed are they which do hunger and
thirst after righteousness."*

I think I must have astonished some who have
been mourning and crying, "Oh, that the Lord would
allow me to live upon His righteousness, and I would
thank Him forever and ever!" Why, you are one of
the blessed. "Alas!" cries one, "I am pining to be delivered from sin—I do not mean from the punishment of it, but from the taint of it. I want to be
perfectly pure and holy." Do you? My dear friend,
you are numbered among the blessed at this very
moment. A great professing person at your side may
be saying, "Blessed be God, I am perfect already!"
Well, I am not sure about that person's blessedness.
That fine bird is not mentioned in my text, but I am
sure about the soul who hungers and thirsts for
righteousness, for the Word is clear and plain:

God Will Bless You

"Blessed are they which do hunger and thirst after righteousness."

SPECIAL SATISFACTION

A Singular Statement

"Blessed are they which do hunger and thirst after righteousness: for they shall be filled." They are to be blessed while they hunger and thirst; if they become filled, will they still be blessed? Yes, and what is more, they will still hunger and thirst. You say that is strange. Yes, it is, but everything is wonderful in the kingdom of God. Paradoxes in spiritual things are as plentiful as blackberries. In fact, if you cannot believe a paradox, you cannot believe in Christ Himself; for He is God and man in one person, and that is a paradoxical mystery. How can one person be infinite, and yet finite? How can He be immortal, and yet die? Ours is a Gospel in which lies many orthodox paradoxes. He who is filled by Christ hungers more than he did before, only the hunger is of another kind and has no bitterness in it. He who hungers most is the man who is full in the highest sense.

Lord, when I get what You give me of Your grace, then I feel a new craving that seeks after higher things! My soul enlarges by what it feeds upon, and then it cries, "Give me still more." When a man stops crying for more, he may doubt whether he has ever received anything at all. Grace fills and then enlarges. Increase of grace is increase of capacity for grace. Cry still, "Lord, increase my faith, my love, my hope, my every grace! Enlarge my soul so that I may take in more and more of You!"

The Righteousness of God

Now I am going to show you how it is that we can be filled even now, although still hungry and thirsty. For first, although we hunger and thirst for righteousness, we are more than filled with the righteousness of God.

I do believe my God to be perfectly righteous, not only in His nature and essence, in His law and judgment, but also in all His decrees, acts, words, and teachings. I sit myself down and anxiously peer into the dreadful truth of the eternal perdition of the wicked, but my heart is full of rest when I remember that God is righteous. The Judge of all the earth must do right. I cannot untie the knots of difficulty over which some men stand perplexed, but I know that God is righteous, and there I leave my bewilderment. God will see to it that the right thing is done in every case, and forevermore. Moreover, as I see how iniquity abounds in the world, I am quite glad that there is no iniquity in the Lord my God.

As I see error in the church, I rest in the fact that no error finds approval with Him. Wrongdoing seems to be everywhere. Certain men would rip away every man's property from him, and the opposite order would grind down the poor in their wages; but this is our main dependence—there is a power that produces righteousness, and that power is God. I am filled with joy as I see righteousness enthroned in God. Do you not know this gladness?

God Will Bless You

The Righteousness of Christ

What if I am sinful? What if I have no righteousness that I dare bring before God? Yet,

> Jesus, thy blood and righteousness
> My beauty are, my glorious dress.

True, I have to cry with the leper, "Unclean, unclean"; and yet, as a believer in the Lord Jesus, I am justified in Him, accepted in Him, and complete in Him. God looks on me, not as I am, but as Christ is. He sees me through the perfect obedience of the Well-beloved, and I stand before Him without condemnation—more than that, with full acceptance and favor. The more you think of the righteousness of Christ, the more it will fill you with grateful satisfaction, for His righteousness is far greater than your unrighteousness. Yet, you will be crying all the same, "O Lord, perfect me in Your image, and give me righteousness!" A fullness of divine contentment, even to running over, will be yours while you sing, *"There is therefore now no condemnation to them which are in Christ Jesus"* (Rom. 8:1). *"Therefore being justified by faith, we have peace with God through our Lord Jesus Christ"* (5:1).

You will be satisfied, first, with the righteous character of God, and next, with the plan of divine righteousness revealed in Christ Jesus. Look at the sin of this world, and groan over it. What a wicked world it is! Read of wars and oppressions, falsehoods and superstitions, or, if you prefer it, see with your own eyes the slums of East London or the iniquity of the great folks in West London; then you will hunger and thirst. But even concerning all this you will be filled as you think of the Atonement of Christ and remember that it is more sweet to God than the fact that all the sin of man is nauseous. The sweet savor of His sacrifice has removed from the thrice-holy God the reek of this dunghill world, and He no longer says that He is sorry that He has made man upon the earth. (See Genesis 6:6.) Because of Christ's righteousness, the Lord God bears with guilty man and still waits so that He may be gracious to the earth and make it anew in Christ Jesus.

The Righteousness That the Holy Spirit Works

I am not saying here that those who are blessed in this way are satisfied to remain as they are, but they are very grateful for what they are. I am a sinner, but yet I do not love sin. Is this not delightful? Though I have to fight daily against corruption, I have received an inner life that will fight, must fight, and will not be conquered. If I have not yet vanquished sin, it is something to be struggling against it. Even now, by faith we claim the victory. *"Thanks be to God, which giveth us the victory through our Lord Jesus Christ"* (1 Cor. 15:57).

Have you ever felt as if you were full to the brim, when you knew that you were *"begotten ...again unto a lively hope by the resurrection of Jesus Christ from the dead"* (1 Pet. 1:3)? Have you not been filled with delight to know that you were no longer what you used to be, but that you were now made a partaker of the divine nature and elevated into the spiritual sphere, where you have fellowship with *"just men made perfect"* (Heb. 12:23)? Never despise what the Holy Spirit has done for you; never undervalue grace already received; but, on the contrary, feel a divine delight, a filling-up of your heart, with what the Lord has already done. Perfection lies in embryo within your soul; all that you are yet to be is there in the seed. Heaven slumbers in repentance, like an oak within an acorn. Glory be to God for a new heart! Glory be to God for life from the dead! Here we are filled with thankfulness, and yet we go on hungering and thirsting so that the blessing that God has given may be more fully enjoyed in our experiences and more fully displayed in our lives.

FILLED WITH RIGHTEOUSNESS

Believers, I can tell you when we get filled with righteousness, and that is when we see righteousness increasing among our fellowmen. The sight of one poor child converted has filled my heart for a week with unspeakable joy. I have talked frequently with poor people who have been great sinners, and the Lord has made them great saints. Then, I have been as filled with happiness as a man could be. A dozen conversions have set all the bells of my heart ringing marriage peals and kept them at it for months on end.

It is true that I might have remembered with sadness the multitudes of sinners who are still perishing, and this would have made me go on hungering and thirsting as I do, but still a dozen or two conversions have seemed so rich a blessing that I have been filled with joy even to overflowing. Then I have felt like good old Simeon, when he said, *"Lord, now lettest thou thy servant depart in peace...for mine eyes have seen thy salvation"* (Luke 2:29–30). Do you not know what this means? Perhaps not, if you are a big man and must do everything on a big scale, but for a poor soul like me, it has been heaven enough to save a single soul from death. I reckon it a great reward to save a little child. It is bliss to me to bring a humble workingman to the Lord's feet and see him learning the way of righteousness.

Oh, try it, beloved! Try and see if hunger for the souls of men will not be followed by a fullness of delight, which will again lead on to further hunger to bring back lost sheep to Christ's fold. You will never say, "I have had many conversions, and therefore I am satisfied to have no more." No, the more you succeed, the more you will hunger and thirst that Christ's kingdom may come in the hearts of the sons of Adam.

By and by we will leave this mortal body, and we will find ourselves in the disembodied state, forever with the Lord. We will have no ears and eyes, but our spirits will discern and understand without these dull organs. Set free from this material substance, we will know no sin. Soon the resurrection trumpet will sound, and the spirit will enter the refined and spiritualized body, and perfected humanity will be ours. Then the man will have his eyes, but they will never cast a lustful glance; he will have his ears, but they will never long for unclean talk; he will have his lips, but they will never lie; he will have a heart that will always beat truly and obediently. There will be nothing amiss within his perfected being. Oh, what a heaven that will be to us! I protest that I want no other heaven than to be with Christ and to be like Him. Harps for music and crowns for honor are little when compared with *"the kingdom of God, and his righteousness"* (Matt. 6:33).

Then we will be filled with righteous society. You will not have to watch your tongue, for fear somebody should make you an offender because of a word. You will not be plagued with idle chitchat and silly gossip when you get to heaven. You will hear no lying there; you will hear nothing that takes away from the infinite majesty of the Most High. Everybody will be perfect. Oh, will you not delight yourself in the abundance of righteousness?

And then, your Lord will descend from heaven with a shout, the dead in Christ will rise, and He will reign with them upon the earth, King of Kings and Lord of Lords. Then will come a thousand years of perfect peace, rest, joy, and glory, and you will be there. What wonderful swimming in a sea of righteousness will be yours! You will then be like Christ in all things, and all your surroundings will agree with that. Heaven and earth will link hands in righteousness. Eternity will follow with its unbroken blessedness. There will be no impurity in the kingdom of the blessed God. No Devil to tempt, no flesh to corrupt, no need to worry, nothing to disturb; but you will be,

> Far from a world of grief and sin,
> With God eternally shut in.

Oh, this is what it means to be filled with righteousness!

The Hunger and Thirst That Are Blessed

My readers, you will never be filled unless you hunger first. You must hunger and thirst here so that you may be filled hereafter. If you are hungering and thirsting, what should you do? Look to Jesus, for He alone can satisfy you. Believe on our Lord Jesus Christ. Believe on Him now, for He is made of God unto us righteousness; and if you want righteousness, you will find it in the Lord Jesus Christ, the only begotten Son of God. "Amen! Amen!" May everybody reading this begin to hunger and thirst for righteousness at once. Let us all say, "Amen!"

6

The Importance of Mercy

Blessed are the merciful: for they shall obtain mercy.
—Matthew 5:7

I have compared the Beatitudes to a ladder of
light in the previous chapters, and I have remarked that every one of them rises above and
out of those that precede it. So you will notice that
the character mentioned here is higher than those
that had been given before, higher than that of the
man who is poor in spirit, or who mourns. Those
things concern himself. He is yet feeble, and out of
this weakness grows a meekness of spirit, which
makes him endure wrongs from others. But to be
merciful is more than that, for the man now not
merely endures wrongs, but he confers benefits.

The beatitude before this one concerns hungering and thirsting for righteousness, but here the
man has gone beyond mere righteousness. He has
risen beyond the seeking of what is right into the
seeking of what is good, kind, generous, and the doing of kind things for his fellowmen. The whole ladder rests upon grace, and grace puts every rung into
its place. It is also grace that, in this place, has
taught the man to be merciful and has blessed him
and given him the promise that he will obtain mercy.

It would be wrong to take any one of these benedictions by itself—for example, to say that every merciful man will obtain mercy or to misquote any other
one in the same way—for that would be to wrest the
Savior's words and to give them a meaning that He
never intended them to convey. Reading the Beatitudes as a whole, we see that this mercifulness, of
which I am about to write, is a characteristic that has
grown out of the rest. It has sprung from all the previous works of grace, and the man is not merely merciful in the human sense, with a humanity that ought
to be common to all mankind, but he is merciful in a
higher and better sense, with a mercy that only the
Spirit of God can ever teach to the soul of man.

Having noticed the rising of this beatitude above
the rest, we will now come to look at it more slowly,
and it is necessary that we should be very guarded
while discussing it. In order to be so, I will ask, first,
who are these blessed people? Secondly, what is their
unique virtue? And, thirdly, what is their special
blessing?

WHO ARE THE MERCIFUL WHO OBTAIN MERCY?

You remember that, at the beginning of this
book, I noted that our Lord's subject when giving the
Beatitudes was not *how* we are to be saved, but *who*
are saved. He is not here describing the way of salvation at all. He does that in many other places, but He
here gives us the signs and evidences of the work of
grace in the soul. So then, we would greatly err if we
said that we must be merciful in order to obtain
mercy, and that we must only hope to get the mercy
of God through first of all being merciful ourselves.

The Importance of Mercy

Now, in order to put aside any such legal notion, which would be quite contrary to the entire current of Scripture and directly opposed to the fundamental doctrine of justification by faith in Christ, I ask you to notice that these persons are blessed already and have already obtained mercy. Long before they became merciful, God was merciful to them. Before the full promise of our text was given to them, that they should obtain yet further mercy, they had already obtained the great mercy of a renewed heart, which had made them merciful. That is clear from the connection of the text.

The Poor in Spirit

It is no common mercy to be emptied of our pride, to be brought to see how undeserving we are in the sight of God, and to be made to feel our personal weakness and need of everything that might make us fit for the presence of God. I could ask no greater mercy for some men, whom I know, than that they might be blessed with spiritual poverty, that they might be made to feel how poor they are. I ask this because these men will never know Christ, and will never rise to be merciful in practice themselves, until they have first seen their own true condition and have obtained mercy enough to lie down at the foot of the cross and there, with a broken heart, to confess that they are empty and poor.

The Mournful

They had mourned over their past sins with bitter repentance; they had mourned over the condition

111

of practical alienation from God into which sin had brought them; and they had mourned over the fact of their ingratitude to their Redeemer, and their rebellion against His Holy Spirit. They mourned because they could not mourn more, and wept because their eyes could not weep as they ought concerning sin. They had

> Learned to weep for nought but sin,
> And after none but Christ.

And it is no small blessing to have the mourning, the broken, the contrite heart, for this the Lord will not despise (Ps. 51:17).

The Gentle and the Meek

They had also become gentle, humble, contented, weaned from the world, and submissive to the Lord's will. They had become ready to overlook the offenses of others, having learned to pray, *"Forgive us our debts, as we forgive our debtors"* (Matt. 6:12), and this is no small blessing. They had indeed obtained mercy when their proud hearts were brought low and their haughty spirits were bowed down, and they had become meek and lowly in measure like their Lord.

Began to Hunger and Thirst for Righteousness

They had obtained yet further grace, for they had a spiritual appetite for the righteousness that is of God by faith. They also had a sacred hunger for the practical righteousness that the Spirit of God works in us. They loved what was right, and they hungered to do it. They hungered to see others do right; they hungered to see the kingdom of righteousness established and the truth of God prevailing over all the earth. Was not this to obtain mercy indeed? And, if out of this grew the character of being merciful, it was not to be ascribed to anything in themselves or regarded as a natural outgrowth of their own dispositions, but as another gift of grace, another fruit, that grew out of special fruits that had already been given.

Was it not already said of these people, *"Theirs is the kingdom of heaven"* (Matt. 5:3)? Had they not obtained mercy? Was it not said of them, *"They shall be comforted"* (v. 4)? Who dare say they had not obtained mercy? Had it not been said of them, *"They shall inherit the earth"* (v. 5)? What do you call this but mercy? Had not the voice of Christ declared, *"They shall be filled"* (v. 6)? Was this not mercy to the fullest extent? Therefore, I say that the people our text speaks of were a people who had already obtained mercy, who were themselves individual trophies of mercy, and the fact that they displayed mercy to others was an inevitable result of what had been done for them and worked in them by the ever-blessed Spirit of God.

They were not merciful because they were naturally tenderhearted, but merciful because God had made them poor in spirit; not merciful because they had compassionate ancestors, but merciful because they themselves had mourned and been comforted. They were not merciful because they sought the esteem of their fellowmen, but because they were themselves meek and lowly and were inheriting the earth and wished that others could enjoy the blessing of heaven as they did. They were not merciful because they could not help it, and felt bound to be so from some constraint from which they would gladly escape, but they were joyfully merciful, for they had hungered and thirsted for righteousness, and they had been filled.

WHAT DOES BEING MERCIFUL INCLUDE?

Kindness to Those in Need

No merciful man could forget the poor. He who passed by their ills without sympathy, and saw their sufferings without relieving them, might chatter as he would about inward grace, but there could not be grace in his heart. The Lord does not acknowledge as one of His family someone who can see his brother in need and shut up *"his bowels of compassion from him"* (1 John 3:17). The apostle John rightly asked, *"How dwelleth the love of God in him?"* (v. 17). No, the truly merciful are considerate of those who are poor.

The truly merciful think of those less fortunate. Their own comforts make them think of them; at other times, their own discomforts will make them think so. When they are sick and they are surrounded with much help and comfort, they wonder how those who are sick and in poverty fare as well. When the wind is sharp around them and their garments are warm, they think with pity of those who shiver in the same cold but are scantily covered with rags. Their sufferings and their joys alike help them to consider the poor.

The Importance of Mercy

They consider them practically. They do not madly say that they sympathize and hope others will help, but they give of their substance according to their ability, joyfully and cheerfully, so that the poor may not lack. In dealing with them, they are not hard. They will remit, as far as they can justly do so, anything they may have demanded of them and will not persecute them to the utmost extremity, as those do who seek to obtain the last morsel and the uttermost penny from the poorest of the poor. No, where God has given a man a new heart and a right spirit, there is great tenderness to all the poor, and especially great love to the poor saint. This is because, while every saint is an image of Christ, the poor saint is a picture of Christ set in the same frame in which Christ's picture must always be set—the frame of humble poverty. I see much in a rich saint that is like his Maker, but I do not see how he could truthfully say, "I have nowhere to lay my head." (See Matthew 8:20.) Nor do I wish him to say it, but when I see poverty, as well as everything else that is like Christ, I think I am bound to feel my heart especially going forth there.

By caring for the poorest of His people, we can still wash Christ's feet. This is how honorable women can still minister to Him of their substance. This is how we can still make a great feast to which we may invite Him: when we call together the poor, the lame, and the blind, who cannot recompense us, and we are content to do it for Jesus Christ's sake. It is said of Chrysostom that he so continually preached the doctrine of almsgiving in the Christian church that they called him "the preacher of alms," and I think it is not a bad title for a man to wear.

God Will Bless You

In these days, it has almost become a crime to relieve the poor; in fact, I do not know whether there are not some statutes that might almost render us liable to prosecution for it. I can only say that the spirit of the times may be wise under some aspects, but it does not seem to me to be very clearly the spirit of the New Testament. The poor will never cease to be in the land, and the poor will never cease to be in the true church of Christ. They are Christ's legacy to us. It is quite certain that the Good Samaritan got more out of the poor man whom he found between Jerusalem and Jericho than the poor man got out of him. The poor man got a little oil and wine and enough money to cover the expenses at the inn. But the Samaritan got his name into the Bible, and there it has been handed down to posterity—a wonderfully cheap investment. In everything that we give, the blessing comes to those who give it, for you know the words of the Lord Jesus, how He said, *"It is more blessed to give than to receive"* (Acts 20:35). Blessed are they who are merciful to the poor.

Compassion for Mourners

The worst ill in the world is not poverty; the worst of ills is a depressed spirit. At least, I scarcely know anything that can be worse than this, and there are even among the excellent of the earth some who seldom have a bright day in the whole year. December seems to rule the whole twelve months. Because of their heaviness, they are subject to bondage all their lives long. If they march to heaven, it is on crutches as Mr. Ready-to-halt did, and they water the way with tears as Miss Much-afraid did in Bunyan's *The Pilgrim's Progress*. They are afraid sometimes that they were never converted; at another time, that they have fallen from grace; at another time, that they have sinned the unpardonable sin; at another time, that Christ has left them, and they will never see His face again. They are full of all kinds of troubles; *"they reel to and fro, and stagger like a drunken man, and are* [often] *at their wit's end"* (Ps. 107:27).

There are many Christian people who always get out of the way of such folks as these, or if they come across them, they say, "It is enough to make anybody miserable. Who wants to talk with such people? They ought not to be so sad; they really ought to be more cheerful; they are giving way to nervousness," and so on. That may be quite true, but it is always a pity to say it. You might as well tell a man when he has a headache that he in giving way to the headache, or when he has a fever that he is giving way to the fever. The fact is, there is nothing more real than some of those diseases that are traceable to the imagination, for they are real in their pain, though perhaps we could not reason about them as to their causes.

The merciful man is always merciful to these people. He puts up with their whims. He knows very often that they are very foolish, but he understands that he would be foolish too if he were to tell them so, for it would make them more foolish than they are. He does not consult his own comfort and say, "I want to get comfort from this person"; he desires to confer comfort. He remembers that it is written, *"Strengthen ye the weak hands, and confirm the feeble knees"* (Isa. 35:3), and he knows that command, *"Comfort ye, comfort ye my people, saith your God. Speak ye comfortably to Jerusalem"* (Isa. 40:1–2). He understands that, as his Lord and Master sought after what was wounded, bound up what was broken, healed what was sick, and brought in what was driven away, in the same way all His servants should imitate their Master by looking with greatest interest after those who are in the saddest plight.

O children of God, if ever you are hardhearted toward any sorrowful person, you are not what you ought to be. You are not like your Master; you are not like yourselves when you are in your right state of mind, for when you are, you are tender and full of pity and compassion. You have learned from the Lord Jesus that the merciful are blessed and that they will obtain mercy. Possibly, when you too become depressed, as you may, you may recollect those jeering words and those unkind expressions that you used concerning others. When we get very big, it may be that the Lord will take us down, and we will be glad for any little mouse holes to hide our heads in.

Some of us have known what it is to be glad of the very least promise, if we could but get a hold of it. We have run with eagerness to the very texts we used to point poor sinners to, and we felt they were just the very verses we wanted. Dr. Guthrie, when he was very ill and about to die, said he liked to hear the little children's hymns, and the strongest men in the family of Christ often want the children's texts and the children's promises. Even the little children's promises suit big men when they are in that sad state. *"Be ye therefore merciful, as your Father also is merciful"* (Luke 6:36), toward those who are cast down.

Full Forgiveness

"Blessed are the merciful," that is, those persons who do not take to heart any injuries that are done them, any insults, intended or unintended. A certain governor of Georgia, in Mr. Wesley's day, said that he would have his servant on board his vessel flogged for drinking his wine. When Mr. Wesley entreated that the man might be pardoned on that occasion, the governor said, "It is no use, Mr. Wesley; you know, sir, I never forgive."

"Well, then, sir," said Mr. Wesley, "I hope you know that you will never be forgiven, or else I hope that you have never sinned."

So, until we stop sinning, we must never talk of not forgiving other people, for we need forgiveness for ourselves. You will notice in many families that quarrels arise even between brothers and sisters, but let us always be ready to put aside anything that will make discord or cause ill feeling, for a Christian is the last person who should harbor unkind thoughts.

I have occasionally noticed great severity toward servants who are sometimes thrown out of jobs and exposed to many temptations for a fault that might be cured if it were forgiven and if some kind word were used. It is not right for any one of us to say, "I will have everybody acting fairly toward me, and I will let everyone know it; I am determined to stand no nonsense, not I! I mean to have the right thing done by all men toward me, and if not, I will set them right." Ah, dear friends, God never talked so to you, and let me also mention, if that is the way you talk, it is not the language of a child of God at all. A child of God feels that he is himself imperfect and that he lives with imperfect people; when they act improperly toward him, he feels it, but at the same time he also feels, "I have been far worse to my God than they have been to me, so I will let it go by."

I recommend, dear brothers and sisters, that you always have one blind eye and one deaf ear. I have always tried to have them; and my blind eye is the best eye I have, and my deaf ear is the best ear I have. There are many speeches that you may hear even from your best friends that would cause you much grief and produce much ill; so do not hear them. They will probably be sorry that they spoke so unkindly if you never mention it and let the whole thing die, but if you say something about it, bring it up again and again, fret and worry over it, magnify it, tell somebody else about it, and bring a half dozen people into the quarrel, that is the way family disagreements have been made, Christian churches broken up, the Devil magnified, and God dishonored. Oh, do not let it be so with us, but let us feel, if there is any offense against us, *"Blessed are the merciful,"* and such we mean to be.

Great Mercy toward Great Sinners

However, this mercifulness goes much further. The Pharisee had no mercy upon the man who was a publican. "Well," said he, "if he has sunk down so low as to collect the Roman tax from his fellow subjects, he is a disgraceful fellow. He may get as far away as he possibly can from my dignified self." And as for the harlot, it did not matter: though she might be ready to shed enough tears to wash her Savior's feet, she was a polluted vessel, and Christ Himself was looked upon as being polluted because He allowed a woman who had been a sinner to show her repentance and her love in such a manner.

Simon and the other Pharisees felt, "Such people have put themselves out of the pale of society, and let them stay there. If they have gone astray like that, let them suffer for it," and there is much of that spirit still in this hypocritical world, for a great part of the world is a mass of the most awful hypocrisy that one can imagine. There are men who are living in vile sin; they know they are, and yet they go into society and are received as if they were the most respectable persons in the world. However, should it so happen that some poor woman is led astray, she is much too vile for these gentlemen to know anything about her existence. The scoundrels, to have an affectation of virtue while they are themselves indulging in the grossest vice! Yet it is so, and there is a prudery about society that says at once, "Oh, we hold up our hands in horror at anybody who has done anything at all wrong against society or the laws of the land."

Now, a Christian thinks far harder things of sin than a worldly person does. He judges sin by a much sterner rule than other men do, but he always thinks kindly of the sinner. If he could, he would lay down his life to reclaim the sinner, as his Master did before him. He does not say, "Stand by yourself; do not come near to me, for I am holier than you," but he considers it to be his chief concern on earth to cry to sinners, *"Behold the Lamb of God, which taketh away the sin of the world"* (John 1:29). So the merciful Christian is not one who shuts anybody out; he is not one who thinks anyone beneath his notice; he would be glad if he could bring to Jesus the most fallen and the most depraved. We honor these dear Christians who are the most completely occupied in this holy work, for the lower they have to go, the greater their honor is in the sight of God, in being permitted thus to rake the very kennels of sin to find precious gems for Christ. Surely, the brightest gems in His crown will come out of the darkest and foulest places where sinners have been lost. *"Blessed are the merciful"* who care for the fallen, for those who have gone astray, *"for they shall obtain mercy."*

Mercy on the Souls of All Men

The merciful man does not care merely for the extremely fallen class, so called by the men of the world, but he regards the whole race as fallen. He knows that all men have gone astray from God, and that all are shut up in sin and unbelief until eternal mercy comes to their deliverance; therefore, his pity goes forth toward the respectable, the rich, and the great, and he often pities princes and kings because they have so few to tell them the truth. He pities the poor rich, for while there are efforts made for the reclaiming of the working classes, how few efforts are ever made for the reclaiming of dukes and duchesses, and for bringing such big sinners as the "Right Honorables" to know Jesus Christ! He feels pity for them, and he feels pity for all nations—the nations that sit in heathen darkness. He longs that grace would come to all, that the truths of the Gospel would be proclaimed in every street, and that Jesus would be made known to every son and daughter of Adam. He has a love for them all.

I pray for you, fellow believers, never to trifle with this true instinct of the newborn nature. The great doctrine of election is very precious to us, and we hold it most firmly, but there are some—and it must not be denied—who allow that doctrine to chill their love toward their fellowmen. They do not seem to have much zeal for their conversion and are quite content to sit down or stand by idly, yet they believe that the decrees and purposes of God will be fulfilled. So they will, but it will be through warm-hearted Christians who bring others to Jesus. The Lord Jesus will *"see of the travail of his soul"* (Isa. 53:11), but it will be by one who is saved telling of salvation to another, and that other to a third, and so on until the sacred fire spreads, until the earth will be surrounded with its flame.

The Christian is merciful to all and anxiously longs that they may be brought to know the Savior, and he makes efforts to reach them. To the utmost of his ability, he tries to win souls to Jesus. He also prays for them. If he is really a child of God, he takes time to plead with God for sinners, and he gives what he can to help others spend their time in telling sinners the way of salvation and in pleading with them as ambassadors for Christ. The Christian man makes this one of his great delights, if by any means he may, by the power of the Spirit, turn a sinner from the error of his ways and so save a soul from death and hide a multitude of sins (James 5:20).

God Will Bless You

Merciful Desires for the Good of God's Creatures

I have many more things to say about this mercifulness. It is so wide a subject that I cannot give all its details. It certainly means a love for all of God's creatures, even the lowliest. The merciful man is merciful to his beast. I do not believe in the piety of a man who is cruel to a horse. There is need of the whip sometimes, but the man who uses it cruelly cannot surely be a converted man.

There are sights to be seen sometimes in our streets that may well provoke the God of heaven to come down in indignation and punish the cruelty of brutal persons to brute beasts. But where the grace of God is in our hearts, we would not cause unnecessary pain to a fly. If, in the course of the necessities of mankind, pain must be given to the inferior animals, the Christian heart is pained and will try to devise all possible means to prevent any unnecessary pain from being endured by a single creature that God's hand has made. There is some truth in that saying of the ancient mariner in Coleridge's "Rime of the Ancient Mariner": "He prayeth well, who loveth well both man and bird and beast." There is a touch, if it is not always of grace, of something like grace in the kindness of heart that every Christian should feel toward all the living things that God has made.

Mercy for Others' Characters

Further, the merciful man shows his mercy to his fellowmen in many ways of this kind. He is merciful in not believing a great many reports he hears about reputed good men. He is told some astonishing story that is very slanderous to the character of a Christian brother, and he says, "Now, if that brother were told this story about me, I would not like him to believe it of me unless he searched it out and was quite sure of it, and I won't believe it of him unless I am forced to do so." It is a delightful thing for Christians to have confidence in others' characters. Wherever that rules in a church, it will prevent a world of sorrow.

Christian, I have more confidence in you than I can ever have in myself, and as I can truly say that, you should be able to say the same of your fellow Christian, too. Do not be ready to receive such reports; there is as much wickedness in believing a lie as in telling it, if we are always ready to believe it. There would be no slanderers if there were no receivers and believers of slander, for when there is no demand for an article, there are no producers of it. If we will not believe evil reports, the talebearer will be discouraged and stop his evil trade. But suppose we are compelled to believe it? Then the merciful man shows his mercy by not repeating it. "Alas," he says, "it is true, and I am very sorry, but why should I publish it abroad?" If there happened to be a traitor in a regiment, I do not think the other soldiers would go and publish it everywhere and say, "Our regiment has been dishonored by one of our comrades." The saying goes, "It is an ill bird that fouls its own nest," and it is an ill-professing Christian who uses his tongue to tell the faults and failures of his brothers.

Suppose we have heard such a tale; the merciful man feels it his duty not to repeat it. Many a man has been ruined for life through some fault that he committed when young, which has been severely dealt with. A young man has misappropriated a sum of money and has been brought before the magistrates and put in jail, and so made a thief for life. Forgiveness for the first action, with prayer and kindly rebuke, might have won him to a life of virtue or—who knows?—to a life of piety. It is for the Christian, at any rate, not to expose someone, unless it is absolutely necessary, as sometimes it is, but always to deal with the erring in the gentlest manner possible.

And, we should be merciful to one another in seeking never to look at the worst side of a brother's character. Oh, how quick some are to spy out other people's faults! They hear that Mr. So-and-so is very useful in the church, and they say, "Yes, he is, but he has a very curious way of going to work, has he not? And he is so eccentric." Well, did you ever know a good man who was very successful who was not a little eccentric? Some people are too smooth ever to do much; it is the odd qualities about us that are the force of our characters, but why be so quick to point out all our flaws?

Do you go out, when the sun is shining brightly, and say, "Yes, this sun is a very good illuminator, but I must say that it has spots"? If you do, you had better keep your remark to yourself, for the sun gives more light than you do, whatever spots you may or may not have. Many excellent people in the world have spots, but yet they do good service for God and for their fellowmen. So, let us not always be the spot finders. Let us look at the bright side of the brother's character, rather than the dark one, and feel that we rise in reputation when other Christians rise in reputation. Let us know that, as they have honor through their holiness, our Lord has the glory of it, and we share in some of the comfort of it. Let us never join in the loud outcries that are sometimes raised against people who may have committed very small offenses.

Many times we have heard men cry, their voices sounding like the baying of a pack of hounds, against some man for a mistaken judgment or what was little more, "Down with him; down with him!" And if he happens to get into some financial trouble at the same time, then he must surely be a worthless fellow; for lack of money is with some men a clear proof of the lack of virtue, and lack of success in business is regarded by some as the most damning of all vices. But, may we be delivered from such outcries against good men who make mistakes, and may our mercy always take the shape of being willing to restore to our love and to our society any who may have erred but who, nevertheless, show hearty and true repentance and a desire from this point on to adorn the doctrine of God their Savior in all things! You who are merciful will be ready to receive your prodigal brother when he comes back to his Father's house. Do not be like the elder brother, and when you hear the music and the dancing ask, "What do these things mean?" But, count it proper that all should be glad when he who was lost is found, and he who was dead is made alive again.

Protecting Others from Temptation

You know that there is such a thing as exposing our young people to temptation. Parents will sometimes allow their children to start life in houses where there is a chance of rising but where there is a greater chance of falling into great sin. They do not appraise the moral risks that they sometimes run by putting their children into large houses where there is no regard for morals, and where there are a thousand nets of Satan spread to take unwary birds. Be merciful to your children; do not let them be exposed to evils that were, perhaps, too strong for you in your youth and that will be too powerful for them. Let your mercy consider them, and do not put them in that position.

As to your clerks and others who work with you, we are sometimes, when we have dishonest people around us, about as guilty as they are. We did not lock up our money and take proper care of it. If we had done so, they could not have stolen it. We leave things lying around sometimes, and through our carelessness the suggestion may often come, "May I not take this and take that?" And so, we may be partakers in their sins through our own lack of care. Remember, they are only men and women— sometimes they are only boys and girls—and do not put baits before them. Keep temptation from them as much as you can.

Not Demanding Too Much from Others

I believe there are persons who demand those who work for them to toil twenty-four hours a day or around that. No matter how hard the task, it never strikes them that their workers' heads ache, or that their legs grow weary. "What were they made for but to slave for us?" That is the kind of notion some have, but that is not the notion of a true Christian. He feels that he desires his workers to do their duty, and he is grieved to find that many of them cannot be made to do that. However, when he sees them diligently doing it, he often feels for them even more than they feel for themselves, for he is considerate and gentle. Who likes to drive a horse the extra mile that makes the creature feel ready to drop? Who would wish to get out of his fellowman that extra hour of work, which is just what makes him wretched? I will put all that I have said into one sentence: let us, dear friends, be tender, considerate, kind, and gentle to all.

"Oh," says one, "if we were to go about the world acting like that, we would get imposed upon; we would get badly treated," and so on. Well, try it, brother; try it, sister; and you will find that any misery that comes to you through being too tenderhearted, too gentle, and too merciful will be so light an affliction that it will not be worthy to be compared with the peace of mind that it will bring you and the constant wellspring of joy that it will put into your own heart as well as into the hearts of others.

THE BLESSING PROMISED TO THE MERCIFUL

It is said of them that, *"they shall obtain mercy."* I cannot help believing that this means in this present life as well as in the life to come. Surely this is David's meaning in the forty-first Psalm: *"Blessed is he that considereth the poor: the LORD will deliver him in time of trouble....He shall be blessed upon the earth"* (vv. 1–2). Is that text gone altogether under the new dispensation? Are those promises only meant for the old legalistic times! We have the sun, but remember that when the sun shines, the stars are shining too. We do not see them because of the greater brightness, but every star is shining in the day, as well as in the night, and increasing the light. And so, though the greater promises of the Gospel sometimes make us forgot the promises of the old dispensation, they are not canceled. They are still there, and they are confirmed, and they are made yea and amen in Christ Jesus to the glory of God by us (2 Cor. 1:20).

I firmly believe that when a man is in trouble, if he has been enabled through divine grace to be kind and generous toward others, he may look to God in prayer and say, "Lord, there is Your promise; I claim no merit for it, but Your grace has enabled me to help others when I saw them in the same condition as I am. Lord, raise up a helper." Job seemed to get some comfort out of that fact. It is not our grandest comfort or our best. As I have said, it is not the sun; it is only one of the stars. At the same time, we do not despise the starlight. I believe that God will quite often help and bless, in temporal matters, those persons whom He has blessed with a merciful spirit toward others.

Often, it is true in another sense that those who have been merciful obtain mercy, for they obtain mercy from others. Our Savior said,

Give, and it shall be given unto you; good measure, pressed down, and shaken together, and running over, shall men give into your bosom. For with the same measure that ye mete withal it shall be measured to you again.
(Luke 6:38)

There will be this sort of general feeling. If a man was sternly just, and no more, when he comes down in the world, few pity him; but all say about that other man, when he is found in trouble, whose earnest endeavor it was to be the helper of others, "We are so sorry for him."

The full meaning of the text, no doubt, relates to that day of which Paul wrote concerning his friend, Onesiphorus: *"The Lord grant unto him that he may find mercy of the Lord in that day"* (2 Tim. 1:18). Do not think that I am building up mercy as a meritorious work; I did my best at the outset to put all that aside. But, as an evidence of grace, mercy is a very prominent and distinguishing mark, and if you want proof of that, let me remind you that our Savior's own description of the Day of Judgment was this:

> *Then shall the King say unto them on his right hand, Come, ye blessed of my Father, inherit the kingdom prepared for you from the foundation of the world: for I was an hungered, and ye gave me meat: I was thirsty, and ye gave me drink: I was a stranger, and ye took me in: naked, and ye clothed me: I was sick, and ye visited me: I was in prison, and ye came unto me.* *(Matt. 25:34–36)*

This, therefore, is evidence that they were blessed of the Father.

7

Having a Pure Heart

Blessed are the pure in heart: for they shall see God.
—Matthew 5:8

It was a unique quality of the great Apostle and High Priest of our profession, Jesus Christ our Lord and Savior, that His teaching was continually aimed at the hearts of men. Other teachers had been content with outward moral reformation, but He sought the source of all evil so that He might cleanse the spring from which all sinful thoughts, words, and actions come. He insisted over and over again that, until the heart was pure, the life would not be clean.

The memorable Sermon on the Mount, from which our text is taken, begins with the benediction, *"Blessed are the poor in spirit"* (Matt. 5:3), for Christ was dealing with men's spirits—with their inner, spiritual nature. He did this more or less in all the Beatitudes, and the one that makes up the text for this chapter strikes the very center of the target since He did not say, "Blessed are the pure in language or the pure in action," much less, "Blessed are the pure in ceremonies, in rules, or in food"; but *"Blessed are the pure in heart."*

O beloved, no matter what so-called "religion" may recognize as its adherent a man whose heart is impure, the religion of Jesus Christ will not do so. His message to all men still is, *"Ye must be born again"* (John 3:7); that is to say, the inner nature must be divinely renewed or else you cannot enter or even see the kingdom of God that Christ came to set up in this world. If your actions should appear to be pure, yet, if the motive at the back of those actions should be impure, that will nullify them all. If your language should be chaste, yet, if your heart is reveling in foul imaginations, you stand before God not according to your words, but according to your desires. According to the set of the current of your affections, your real inward likes and dislikes, you will be judged by Him. External purity is all that man asks at our hands, *"for man looketh on the outward appearance, but the LORD looketh on the heart"* (1 Sam. 16:7), and the promises and blessings of the covenant of grace belong to those who are made pure in heart, and to none besides.

In writing about this text, I want to show you, first, that impurity of heart is the cause of spiritual blindness; secondly, that the purification of the heart admits us to a most glorious sight: *"the pure in heart...shall see God."* Then I will have to show you, in the third place, that the purification of the heart is a divine operation that cannot be performed by ourselves or by any human agency, but must be worked by Him who is the holy triune God.

IMPURITY OF HEART CAUSES SPIRITUAL BLINDNESS

A man who is intoxicated cannot see clearly; his vision is often distorted or doubled. There are other cups, besides those which intoxicate, that prevent the mental eye from having clear sight, and he who has once drunk deeply of these cups will become spiritually blind. Others, in proportion as they take in the unwholesome drinks, will be unable to see afar off.

Unseen Beauties and Horrors

There are moral beauties and immoral horrors that those who are impure cannot see. Take, for instance, the covetous man, and you will soon see that there is no other dust that blinds so completely as gold dust. There is a trade that many regard as bad from top to bottom, but if it pays the man who is engaged in it, and he is of a grasping disposition, it will be almost impossible to convince him that it is an evil trade.

You will usually find that the covetous man sees no charm in generosity. He thinks that the generous man, if he is not actually a fool, is so near akin to one that he might very easily be mistaken for one. He himself admires what can be most easily grasped, and the more of it that he can secure, the better he is pleased. Cheating people and oppressing the poor are occupations in which he takes delight. If he has performed a dirty trick in which he has sacrificed every principle of honor, but, if it has turned out to his own advantage, he says to himself, "That was a clever stroke." If he meets with another man of his own kind, he and his friend would chuckle over the transaction and say how beautifully they had done it. It would be useless for me to attempt to reason with a mercenary man, to show him the beauty of generosity, and, on the other hand, I would not think of wasting my time in trying to get from him a fair opinion as to the justice of anything that he knew to be profitable.

You know that there was a great fight in the United States over the question of slavery. Who were the gentlemen in England who took the side of the slave owners? Why, mostly Liverpool men, who did so because slavery paid them. If it had not done so, they would have condemned it, and I suppose that those of us who condemned it did so more readily because it did not pay us. Men can see very clearly when there is nothing to be lost either way, but if it comes to be a matter of gain, the eyes cannot see straight when the heart is impure. There are innumerable things that a man cannot see if he holds a gold coin over each of his eyes—he cannot even see the sun then—and if he keeps the gold over his eyes, he will become blind. The pure in heart can see, but when covetousness gets into the heart, it makes the eyes dim or blind.

Take another sin—the sin of oppression. There are men who tell us that, in their opinion, the persons who are in the highest positions in life are the very beauty and glory of the nation. They also say that poor people ought to be kept in their proper places, because they were created on purpose so that "the nobility" might be sustained in their exalted positions and that other highly respectable persons might also gather any quantity of wealth to themselves. As to the idea of men wanting more money for their services, it ought not to be encouraged for a single moment, so these gentlemen say, and if the poor seamstress toils and starves on the few pennies she can earn, you must not say a word about it. There are "the laws of political economy" that govern all such cases, so she must be ground between the wheels that abound in this age of machinery, and nobody ought to interfere in the matter!

Of course, an oppressor cannot or will not see the evil of oppression. If you put before him a case of injustice that is as plain as the nose on his face, he cannot see it, because he has always been under the delusion that he was sent into the world with a whip in his hand to drive other people about. He is the one great somebody, and other people are poor nobodies, only fit to creep under his huge legs and humbly ask his permission to live. In this way, oppression, if it gets into the heart, completely blinds the eyes and perverts the judgment of the oppressor.

The same remark is true concerning lasciviousness. I have often noticed, when men have railed at religion and reviled the holy Word of God, that their lives have been impure. Seldom, if ever, have I met with a case in which my judgment has deceived me with regard to the lives of men who have spoken against holy things. I remember preaching once in a country town just about harvesttime, and in commenting on the fact that some farmers would not let the poor have any gleanings from their fields, I said I thought there were some who were so stingy that, if they could rake their fields with a fine-tooth comb, they would do so. Immediately after this, a farmer marched noisily out of the place in a fit of indignation, and when he was asked why he was so wrathful, he answered, with the greatest simplicity, "Because I always rake my fields twice." Of course, he could not perceive any particular pleasure in caring for the poor, and neither could he submit with a good grace to the rebuke that came home to him so pointedly.

When men speak against the Gospel, it is almost always because the Gospel speaks against them. The Gospel has found them out; it has charged them with the guilt of their sins and has arrested them. It has come to them like a policeman with his whistle that he has blown loudly because of their iniquity, and therefore it is that they are so indignant. They would not be living as they are if they could see themselves as God sees them; they would not be able to continue in their filthiness, corrupting others as well as ruining themselves, if they could really see. But as these evil things get into the heart, they are certain to blind the eyes.

Regarding Spiritual as Well as Moral Truth

We frequently meet with persons who say that they cannot understand the Gospel of Christ. Behind this, in nine cases out of ten, I believe that it is their sin that prevents their understanding it. For instance, people may say, "We do not recognize the claims of God on us," when presented with His claims. If anyone talks like that, it is because his heart is not right in the sight of God; for if he were able to judge righteously, he would see that the highest claims in all the world are those of the Creator upon His creatures. He would then say at once, "I recognize that He who has created has the right to govern, that He who is both greatest and best should be Master and Lord, and that He who is infallibly wise and just and always kind and good should be Lawgiver." When men practically say, "We would not cheat or rob our fellowmen, but as for God, what does it matter how we treat Him?" the reason is that they are unjust in heart. Their so-called justice to their fellowmen is only because their motto is "Honesty is the best policy," and they are not really just in heart, or else they would at once admit the just claims of the Most High.

The great central doctrine of the Atonement can never be fully appreciated until a man's heart is rectified. You have probably often heard such remarks as these: "I don't see why there should be any payment made to God for sin. Why could He not forgive transgression at once and be done with it? What need is there of a substitutionary sacrifice?" However, if you had ever felt the weight of sin upon your conscience, if you had ever learned to loathe the very thought of evil, if you had been brokenhearted because you have been so terribly defiled by sin, you would feel that the Atonement was not only required by God, but that it was also required by your own sense of justice. Then, instead of rebelling against the doctrine of a vicarious sacrifice, you would open your heart to it and cry, "That is precisely what I need."

The purest-hearted people who have ever lived are those who have rejoiced to see God's righteous law vindicated and magnified by Christ's death upon the cross as the Substitute for all who believe in Him. While God's mercy is displayed in matchless majesty, the pure-hearted people feel the most intense satisfaction that there could be a way of reconciliation by which every attribute of God would derive honor and glory, and yet poor lost sinners would be lifted up into the high and honorable position of children of God. The pure in heart see no difficulty in the Atonement; all the difficulties concerning it arise from the lack of purity in the heart.

The same may be said of the equally important truth of regeneration. The impure in heart cannot see any need of being born again. They say, "We admit that we are not quite all that we should be, but we can easily be made all right. As to the talk about a new creation, we do not see any need of that. We have made a few mistakes, which will be rectified by experience, and there have been some errors of life that we trust may be corrected by future watchfulness and care."

But if the unrenewed man's heart were pure, he would see that his nature had been an evil thing from the beginning. He would realize that thoughts of evil naturally rise in us as sparks fall from a fire, and he would feel that it would be a dreadful thing that such a nature as that would remain unchanged. He would see jealousies, murders, rebellions, and evils of every kind within his heart, and his heart would cry out to be delivered from itself. But just because his heart is impure, he does not see his own impurity and does not and will not confess his need to be made a new creature in Christ Jesus.

As for you who are pure in heart, what do you now think of your old nature? Is it not the heavy burden that you continually carry about with you? Is not the plague of your own heart the worst plague under heaven? Do you not feel that the very tendency to sin is a constant grief to you, and that, if you could only get rid of it altogether, your heaven would have begun below? So it is the pure in heart who see the doctrine of regeneration, and those who do not see it, do not see it because they are impure in heart.

The same remark is true concerning the glorious character of our blessed Lord and Master, Jesus Christ. Who has ever found fault with that, except men with who are blind to the truth? There have been unconverted men who have been struck with the beauty and purity of Christ's life, but the pure in heart are enamored of it. They feel that it is more than a human life, that it is divine, and that God himself is revealed in the person of Jesus Christ His Son. If any man does not see the Lord Jesus Christ to be thus superlatively lovely, it is because he is himself not purified in heart, for if he were, he would recognize in Him the mirror of all perfection and would rejoice to do reverence to Him. But, alas, it is still true that, as it is with moral matters, so is it with that which is spiritual, and therefore the great truths of the Gospel cannot be perceived by those whose hearts are impure.

There is one form of impurity that, beyond all others, seems to blind the eye to spiritual truth, and that is duplicity of heart. A man who is simple-minded, honest, sincere, and childlike is the man who enters the kingdom of heaven when its door is opened to him. The things of the kingdom are hidden from the double-minded and the deceitful, but they are plainly revealed to the babes in grace—the simple-hearted, transparent people who wear their hearts upon their sleeves.

It is quite certain that the hypocrite will never see God while he continues in his hypocrisy. In fact, he is so blind that he cannot see anything, and certainly cannot see himself as he really is in God's sight. The man who is quite satisfied with the name of a Christian without the life of a Christian will never see God or anything at all until his eyes are divinely opened. What does it matter to anybody else what his opinion is upon any subject whatever? We should not care to have praise from the man who is double-minded and who is practically a liar, for, while he is one thing in his heart, he endeavors to pass himself off as another thing in his life.

Formalism, too, will never see God, for formalism always looks to the shell and never gets to the kernel. Formalism licks the bone but never gets to the marrow. It heaps ceremonies on itself, mostly of its own invention, and when it has attended to these, it flatters itself that all is well, though the heart itself still lusts after sin. The widow's house is being devoured even at the very time when the Pharisee is making long prayers in the synagogue or at the street corner. Such a man cannot see God.

There is a kind of reading of the Scriptures that will never lead a man to see God. He opens the Bible, not to see what is there, but to see what he can find to back up his own views and opinions. If the texts he wants are not there, he will twist others around until he gets them on his side somehow or other, but he will only believe what agrees with his own preconceived notions. He would like to mold the Bible, like a cake of wax, to any shape he pleases; so, of course, he cannot see the truth, and he does not want to see it.

The crafty man, too, never sees God. I am afraid for no man as much as for the crafty, the man whose guiding star is "policy." I have seen rough sailors converted to God, and blasphemers, harlots, and great sinners of almost all kinds brought to the Savior and saved by His grace. Very often they have told the honest truth about their sins and have blurted out the sad truth in a very outspoken fashion, and when they have been converted, I have often thought that they were like the good ground of which our Savior spoke (Matt. 13:8, 23), with an honest and good heart in spite of all their badness. But as for the men of snakelike nature, who say to you, when you talk to them about religion, "Yes, yes," but do not mean it at all—the men who are never to be trusted—God Himself never seems to do anything but let them alone. As far as my observation goes, His grace seldom seems to come to these double-minded men who are unstable in all their ways (James 1:8). These are the people who never see God.

A very excellent writer has remarked that our Lord probably alluded to this fact in the verse that forms our text. In Oriental countries, the king is seldom seen. He lives in seclusion, and to get an interview with him is a matter of great difficulty. There are all sorts of plots, plans, intrigues, and perhaps the use of backstairs influence, and in that way a man may at last get to see the king. But Jesus Christ says, in effect, "That is not the way to see God." No one ever gets to Him by craftiness, by plotting, planning, and scheming, but the simple-minded man, who goes humbly to Him, just as he is, and says, "My God, I desire to see You; I am guilty, and I confess my sin and plead with You, for Your dear Son's sake, to forgive it," is the man who sees God.

God Will Bless You

I think there are some Christians who never see God as well as others do—I mean some believers who, from their peculiar constitution, seem naturally of a questioning spirit. They are generally puzzled about some doctrinal point or other, and their time is mostly taken up with answering objections and removing doubts. Perhaps some poor humble countrywoman, who sits in the aisle and who knows, as Cowper says, nothing more than that her Bible is true and that God always keeps His promises, sees a great deal more of God than the learned and quibbling brother who vexes himself about foolish questions to no profit.

I remember a minister who, when calling on an elderly sick woman, desired to leave a passage with her for her private meditation. So, opening her old Bible, he turned to a certain passage, which he found that she had marked with the letter *P*. "What does that *P* mean, my sister?" he asked.

"That means *precious,* sir. I found that text very precious to my soul on more than one special occasion."

He looked for another promise, and next to this he found in the margin *T* and *P*. "And what do these letters mean, my good sister?"

"They mean *tried and proved,* sir, for I tried that promise in my greatest distress and proved it to be true, and then I put that mark next to it so that, the next time I was in trouble, I might be sure that that promise was still true."

The Bible is marked all over with those *T*s and *P*s by generation after generation of believers who have tested the promises of God and proved them to be true. May you and I, beloved, be among those who have thus tried and proved this precious Book!

Having a Pure Heart

THE PURE IN HEART CAN SEE GOD

What does that mean? It means many things; I will briefly mention some of them.

In Nature

When one's heart is clean, he will hear God's footfall everywhere in the garden of the earth in the cool of the day. He will hear God's voice in the storm, sounding in peal on peal from the tops of the mountains. He will behold the Lord walking on the great and mighty waters or see Him in every leaf that trembles in the breeze. Once one gets the heart right, God can be seen everywhere. To an impure heart, God cannot be seen anywhere, but to a pure heart God is to be seen everywhere: in the deepest caverns of the sea, in the lonely desert, in every star that adorns the brow of midnight.

In the Scriptures

Impure minds cannot see any trace of God in the Bible. They see reasons for doubting whether Paul wrote the Epistle to the Hebrews; they doubt the canonicity of the gospel of John, and that is about all that they ever see in the Bible. However, the pure in heart see God on every page of this blessed Book. As they read it devoutly and prayerfully, they bless the Lord that He has been pleased so graciously to reveal Himself to them by His Spirit, and that He has given them the opportunity and the desire to enjoy the revelation of His holy will.

God Will Bless You

In God's Church

The impure in heart cannot see Him there at all. To them, the church of God is nothing but a conglomeration of divided sects, and looking upon these sects, they can see nothing but faults, failures, and imperfections. It should always be remembered that every man sees that which is according to his own nature. When the vulture soars in the sky, it sees the carrion wherever it may be, and when the dove on silver wings mounts up to the azure, it sees the clean winnowed corn wherever it may be. The lion sees its prey in the forest, and the lamb sees its food in the grassy meadow. Unclean hearts see little or nothing of good among God's people, but the pure in heart see God in His church and rejoice to meet Him there.

Discernment of God's True Character

Seeing God means much more than perceiving traces of Him in nature, in the Scriptures, and in His church. Any man who is caught in a thunderstorm, who hears the crash of the thunder, and who sees what havoc the lightning flashes work, perceives that God is mighty. If he is not so foolish as to be an atheist, he says, "How terrible is this God of the lightning and the thunder!" But to perceive that God is eternally just and yet infinitely tender, and that He is sternly severe and yet immeasurably gracious, and to see the various attributes of the Deity all blending into one another as the colors of the rainbow make one harmonious and beautiful whole— this is reserved for the man whose eyes have been first washed in the blood of Jesus and then anointed with heavenly eye salve by the Holy Spirit. It is only such a man who sees that God is always and altogether good and who admires Him under every aspect, seeing that all His attributes are beautifully blended and balanced, and that each one sheds additional splendor upon all the rest. The pure in heart will in that sense see God, for they will appreciate His attributes and understand His character as the ungodly never can.

Admitted into God's Fellowship

When you hear some people talk about there being no God and no spiritual things and so on, you do not need to be at all concerned about what they say, for they are not in a position to guarantee such things in speaking about the matter. For instance, an ungodly man says, "I do not believe there is a God, for I never saw Him." I do not doubt the truth of what you say, but when I tell you that I *have* seen Him, you have no more right to doubt my word than I have to doubt yours.

One day, at a hotel dinner table, I was talking with a fellow minister about certain spiritual things when a gentleman, who sat opposite to us and who had a napkin tucked under his chin and a face that indicated his fondness for wine, made this remark, "I have been in this world for sixty years, and I have never yet been conscious of anything spiritual." We did not say what we thought, but we thought it was very likely that what he said was perfectly true, and there are a great many more people in the world who might say the same as he did. But that only proved that he was not conscious of anything spiritual, not that others were not conscious of it.

There are plenty of other people who can say, "We are conscious of spiritual things. We have been, by God's presence among us, moved and bowed, carried forward and cast down, and then lifted up into joy and happiness and peace. Our experiences are as true phenomena, at least to us, as any phenomena under heaven, and we are not to be beaten out of our beliefs, for they are supported by innumerable undoubted experiences." *"He that dwelleth in the secret place of the most High shall abide under the shadow of the Almighty"* (Ps. 91:1). "But there is no such secret place," says one, "and no such shadow." How do you know that? If someone else comes and says, "Ah! I am dwelling in that secret place and abiding under that shadow," what will you say to him? You may call him a fool if you like, but that does not prove that he is one—though it may prove that you are one—for he is as honest a man as you are and as worthy to be believed as you are.

Some years ago, a lawyer in America attended a religious meeting where he heard approximately a dozen people relating their Christian experience. He sat with his pencil in his hand and jotted down their evidences as they gave them. At last, he said to himself, "If I had a case in court, I would like to have these persons on the witness stand, for I would feel that, if I had their evidence on my side, I would win the case." Then he thought, "Well, I have ridiculed these people as fanatics, yet I would like their evidence in court, upon other matters. They have nothing to gain by what they have been saying, so I ought to believe that what they have said is true." The law-yer was simple enough, or rather, wise enough and pure enough in heart, to look at the matter rightly, and so he also came to see the truth and to see God.

Many of us could testify that there is such a thing as fellowship with God even here on earth, but men can enjoy it only in proportion as they give up their love of sin. They cannot talk with God after they have been talking filthiness. They cannot speak with God as a man speaks with his friend if they are accustomed to meeting merry companions in the tavern and delight to mingle with the ungodly who gather there. The pure in heart may see God, and do see Him, not with the natural eye—far from us is such a carnal idea as that—but with their inner spiritual eye they see the great God who is a Spirit, and they have spiritual but very real communion with the Most High.

The expression, *"they shall see God,"* may mean something else. As I have already said, those who saw Oriental monarchs were generally considered to be highly privileged persons. There were certain ministers of state who had the right to go in and see their king whenever they chose to do so, and the pure in heart have just such a right given to them to go in and see their King at all times. In Christ Jesus, they have boldness and access with confidence in coming to the throne of the heavenly grace. Being cleansed by the precious blood of Jesus, they have become the ministers, that is, the servants of God, and He employs them as His ambassadors and sends them on high and honorable errands for Him. These servants may see Him whenever their business for Him entitles them to an audience with Him.

God Will Bless You

In Heaven

And, lastly, the time will come when those who have thus seen God on earth will see Him face to face in heaven. Oh, the splendor of that vision! It is useless for me to attempt to talk about it. Possibly, within a week, some of us will know more about it than all the theologians on earth could tell us. It is but a thin veil that parts us from the glory world; it may be split apart at any moment, and then at once,

> Far from a world of grief and sin,
> With God eternally shut in,

the pure in heart will fully understand what it is to see God. May that be your portion, beloved, and mine also, forever and ever!

PURIFICATION OF THE HEART IS A DIVINE WORK

In addition to being a divine work, believe me when I tell you that it is never an unnecessary work. No man (except the man Christ Jesus) was ever born with a pure heart. All have sinned; all need to be cleansed. *"There is none...good, no, not one"* (Rom. 3:12).

Never Performed by Any Ceremony

Let me also assure you that men may say what they please, but no application of water ever made a man's heart any better. Some tell us that, in baptism, by which they mean baby sprinkling as a rule, they regenerate and make members of Christ, children of

Having a Pure Heart

God, and inheritors of the kingdom of heaven. But those who are sprinkled are no better than other people; they grow up in just the same way as others. The whole ceremony is useless, and worse that that, for it is completely contrary to the example and teaching of the Lord Jesus Christ. No aqueous applications, no outward ceremonies, can ever affect the heart.

Not by Outward Reformation

The attempt has often been made to work from the outside to the inside, but it cannot be done. You might as well try to give a living heart to a marble statue by working upon the outside of it with a mallet and chisel. To make a sinner pure in heart is as great a miracle as if God were to make that marble statue live, breathe, and walk.

Only by God's Holy Spirit

The Holy Spirit must come upon us and overshadow us, and when He thus comes to us, then our heart is changed, but never before that. When the Spirit of God thus comes to us, He cleanses the soul—to follow the line of our Savior's teaching—by showing us our spiritual poverty: *"Blessed are the poor in spirit"* (Matt 5:3). That is the first work of God's grace, to make us feel that we are poor, that we are nothing, that we are undeserving, ill-deserving, hell-deserving sinners.

As the Spirit of God proceeds with His work, the next thing that He does is to make us mourn: *"Blessed are they that mourn"* (v. 4). We mourn to think that we have sinned as we have done; we mourn after our God; we mourn after pardon; and then the great process that effectually cleanses the heart is the application of the water and the blood that flowed from the torn side of Christ upon the cross. Here it is, O sinners, that you will find a double cure from the guilt and from the power of sin! When faith looks to the bleeding Savior, it sees in Him not merely pardon for the past, but the putting away of the sinfulness of the present. The angel said to Joseph, before Christ was born, *"Thou shalt call his name JESUS: for he shall save his people from their sins"* (Matt. 1:21).

The whole process of salvation may be briefly explained in the following way. The Spirit of God finds us with foul hearts, and He comes and throws a divine light into us so that we see that they are foul. Then He shows us that, being sinners, we deserve to endure God's wrath, and we realize that we do. Then He says to us, "But that wrath was borne by Jesus Christ for you." He opens our eyes, and we see that *"Christ died for us"* (Rom. 5:8)—in our place and instead of us. We look to Him; we believe that He died as our Substitute; and we trust ourselves with Him. Then we know that our sins are forgiven us for His name's sake, and the joy of pardoned sin goes through us with such a thrill as we never felt before.

The next moment, the forgiven sinner cries, "Now that I am saved, now that I am pardoned, my Lord Jesus Christ, I will be Your servant forever. I will put to death the sins that put You to death, and if You will give me the strength to do so, I will serve You as long as I live!" The current of the man's soul ran before toward evil, but the moment that he finds that Jesus Christ died for him and that his sins are forgiven him for Christ's sake, the whole stream of his soul rushes in the other direction toward what is right. Though he still has a struggle against his old nature, from that day forth the man is pure in heart; that is to say, his heart loves purity, his heart seeks after holiness, his heart pines after perfection.

Now he is the man who sees God, loves God, delights in God, longs to be like God, and eagerly anticipates the time when he will be with God and see Him face to face. That is the process of purification; may you all enjoy it through the effectual working of the Holy Spirit! If you are willing to have it, it is freely proclaimed to you. If you truly desire the new heart and the right spirit, they will be graciously given to you. There is no need for you to try to make yourselves fit to receive them. God is able to work them in you this very hour. He who will wake the dead with one blast of the resurrection trumpet can change your nature with the mere volition of His gracious mind. He can, while you read this book, create in you a new heart, renew a right spirit with you (Ps. 51:10), and send you out as different a man from what you were as if you were a newborn child. The power of the Holy Spirit to renew the human heart is boundless.

"Oh," says one, "if only He would renew my heart, if only He would change my nature!" If that is your heart's desire, send up that prayer to heaven now. Do not let the wish die in your soul, but turn it into a prayer and then breathe it out unto God. Listen to what God has to say to you; it is this: *"Come now, and let us reason together, saith the* LORD: *though your sins be as scarlet, they shall be as white as snow; though they be red like crimson, they shall be as wool"* (Isa. 1:18), or this: *"Believe on the Lord Jesus Christ, and thou shalt be saved"* (Acts 16:31). You will be saved from your love of sin, saved from your old habits, and so completely saved that you will become one of the pure in heart who see God.

But, perhaps, you ask, "What is it to believe in the Lord Jesus Christ?" It is to trust Him, to rely upon Him. Oh, that we could all rely upon Jesus Christ now! Oh, that the troubled young man would come and trust in Jesus! You will never get rid of your troubles until you do, but, dear friend, you may be rid of them this very moment if you will but believe in Jesus. Yes, though you have struggled in vain against your evil habits, though you have wrestled with them sternly and resolved and resolved, only to be defeated by your giant sins and your terrible passions, there is One who can conquer all your sins for you. There is One who is stronger than Hercules, who can strangle the persistent evil of your lust, kill the lion of your passions, and cleanse the filthy stable of your evil nature by turning the great rivers of blood and water of His atoning sacrifice right through your soul. He can make and keep you pure within.

Oh, look unto Him! He hung upon the cross, accursed of men, and God made Him to be sin for us, though He knew no sin, that *"we might be made the righteousness of God in him"* (2 Cor. 5:21). He was condemned to die as our Sin-offering in order that we might live forever in the love of God. Trust Him, trust Him! He has risen from the dead and gone up into His glory, and He is at the right hand of God, pleading for transgressors. Trust Him! You can never perish if you do trust Him, but you will live with ten thousand times ten thousand more who have all been saved by grace, to sing of a mighty Savior, able to save to the uttermost all them who come to God by Him (Heb. 7:25). God grant that you may all be saved in this manner, so that you may be among the pure in heart who will see God and never stop seeing Him, and He will have all the glory.

8

Being a Peacemaker

*Blessed are the peacemakers: for they shall be called
the children of God.*
—Matthew 5:9

This is the seventh of the Beatitudes. There is a mystery always connected with the number seven. It was the number of perfection among the Hebrews, and it seems as if the Savior put the peacemaker there, as if such a man was nearly approaching the perfect man in Christ Jesus. He who wants to have perfect blessedness, as far as it can be enjoyed on earth, must labor to attain to this seventh benediction and become a peacemaker.

There is a significance also in the position of the text if you regard the context. The verse that precedes it speaks of the blessedness of *"the pure in heart: for they shall see God"* (v. 8). It is well that we should understand this. We are to be *"first pure, then peaceable"* (James 3:17). Our peaceableness is never to be a compact with sin or an alliance with what is evil. We must set our faces like Him against everything that is contrary to God and His holiness. That being a settled matter in our souls, we can go on to peaceableness toward men.

The verse that follows this text seems to have been put there on purpose as well. However peaceable we may be in this world, we will be misrepresented

157

and misunderstood, and no marvel, for even the
Prince of Peace, by His very peacefulness, brought
fire upon the earth. He Himself, though He loved
mankind and did no evil, was *"despised and rejected of
men; a man of sorrows, and acquainted with grief"*
(Isa. 53:3). Lest, therefore, the peaceable in heart
should be surprised when they meet with enemies, it
is added, in the verse following this chapter's text,
*"Blessed are they which are persecuted for righteous-
ness' sake: for theirs is the kingdom of heaven"* (Matt.
5:10). Thus, the peacemakers are not only pronounced
to be blessed, but they are surrounded with blessings.

Lord, give us grace to climb to this seventh beatitude! Purify our minds that we may be first pure,
then peaceable, and fortify our souls, so that our
peaceableness may not lead us into surprise and despair when, for Your sake, we are persecuted among
men.

Now, let us endeavor to enter into the meaning of
our text. First, let us describe the peacemaker; secondly, let us proclaim his blessedness; thirdly, let us
set him to work; and then, fourthly, let me become a
peacemaker and try to teach you of this blessed peace.

WHO IS THE PEACEMAKER?

The peacemaker, while distinguished by his
character, has the outward position and condition of
other men. He stands in all relations of life just as
other men do.

A Citizen

Though the peacemaker is a Christian, he remembers that Christianity does not require him to

forego his citizenship, but to use and to improve it for Christ's glory. The peacemaker then, as a citizen, loves peace. Though he, like other men, sometimes feels hot blood, he represses it and says to himself, "I must not strive toward war, for the servant of God must *be gentle unto all men, apt to teach, patient'* (2 Tim. 2:24)." So he puts his back against the current, and when he hears the noise of war everywhere and sees many who are eager for it, he does his best to calm them down and says, "Be patient; let it alone; if the thing that might lead to war is an evil, war is worse than any other evil. There was never a bad peace yet, and never a good war." He goes on to say, "Whatever loss we may sustain by being too quiet, we will certainly lose a hundred times as much by being too fierce."

So he says, "What I would not do myself, I would not have others do for me, and if I would not be a killer, neither would I have others killed for me." He walks in vision over a field of battle; he hears the shrieks of the dying and the groans of the wounded; he knows that even conquerors themselves have said that all the enthusiasm of victory has not been able to remove the horror of the dreadful scene after the sight; and so he says, "No! Peace, peace!" If he has any influence in the government, if he is a writer in a newspaper, or if he speaks sometimes in public, he says, "Let us look well into it before we hurry into any strife," when faced with a prospect of war. He says of war that it is a monster, that at its best it is a fiend, that of all scourges it is the worst. He looks upon soldiers as the red twigs of the bloody rod, and he begs God not to smite a guilty nation in this way, but to put away the sword awhile, so that we will not be cast into trouble, overwhelmed with sorrow, and exposed to cruelty, which may bring thousands to the grave and multitudes to poverty. The peace-maker acts in this way, and he feels that while he does so, his conscience justifies him. He is then blessed, and men will one day acknowledge that he was one of the children of God.

A Human Being

If sometimes a peacemaker lets general politics alone, as a human being, he thinks that the politics of his own person must always be those of peace. There, if his honor is stained, he does not stand up for it. He counts that it is a greater stain to his honor for him to be angry with his fellowman than for him to bear an insult. He hears others say, "If you tread upon a worm, it will turn," but he says, "I am not a worm, but a Christian, and therefore I do not turn, except to bless the hand that smites and to pray for those who treat me hatefully." He has his temper, for the peacemaker can be angry, and woe to the man who cannot be! Such a man is like Jacob, limping because of his thigh that the angel touched, for anger is one of the holy feet of the soul, when it goes in the right direction. But while he can be angry, he learns to *"be...angry, and sin not,"* and he does not allow the sun to go down on his wrath (Eph. 4:26).

When he is at home, the peacemaker seeks to be quiet with his family. He puts up with many things sooner than he will speak one improper word. If he scolds someone, it is always with gentleness, saying, "Why do you do this?" not with the severity of a judge, but with the tenderness of a father.

The peacemaker may learn a lesson, perhaps, from a story of Mr. John Wesley, which I alluded to earlier. While going across in a ship to America with Mr. Oglethorpe, who was the governor of Georgia, one day he heard a great noise in the governor's cabin. So Mr. Wesley went there, and the governor said, "I dare say you want to know what this noise is about, sir. I have good occasion for it. You know, sir," said he, "that the only wine I drink is Cyprus wine, and it is necessary for me. I put it on board, and this rascal, my servant, this Grimaldi, has drunk all of it. I will have him beaten on the deck, and he will be taken and enlisted in His Majesty's service by the first ship of war that comes by, and a hard time he will have of it, for I will let him know that I never forgive."

"Your Honor," said Mr. Wesley, "then I hope you never sin."

The rebuke was so well put, so pointed, and so needed, that the governor replied in a moment, "Alas, sir, I do sin, and I have sinned in what I have said; for your sake he will be forgiven. I trust he will not do the same again."

Thus, the peacemaker always thinks that it is best for him, as he is a sinner himself and responsible to his own Master, not to be too hard a master to his servants, for fear that when he is provoking them, he may also be provoking his God.

When the peacemaker is with company, he sometimes meets with slurs, and even with insults, but he learns to bear these, for he remembers that Christ endured many indignities of sinners against Himself. Holy Cotton Mather, a great Puritan clergyman in America, had received a number of anonymous letters in which he was greatly abused. Having read them, he put a piece of paper around them and wrote upon the paper when he put them on a shelf, "Libels—Father, forgive them!" The peacemaker does the same. He says of all these things, "They are libels—Father, forgive them!" and he does not rush to defend himself, knowing that He whom he serves will take care that his good name will be preserved, if only he himself is careful how he walks among men.

While dealing in business, it sometimes happens that the peacemaker is greatly tempted by circumstances to possibly file a lawsuit, but he never does this unless he is directly compelled to do it. He knows that the practice of law is playing with edged tools, and that they who know how to use the tools still cut their own fingers. The peacemaker remembers that the law is most profitable to those who carry it on. He knows, too, that where men will give some small change to the ministry for the good of their souls, and where they pay a few dollars to their physician for the good of their bodies, they will spend a hundred dollars, or five hundred, as a payment to their counsel in the courts. So he says, "No, it is better that I be wronged by my adversary, and he get some advantage, than that both of us should lose our all."

So then, the peacemaker lets some of these things go by, and he finds that on the whole, he is never the loser by sometimes giving up his rights. There are times when he is constrained to defend himself, but even then he is ready for every compromise, willing to give way at any time and at any season. He has learned the old adage, "An ounce of prevention is better than a pound of cure," and so he takes heed to it, agreeing with his adversary quickly while he is yet in the way (Matt. 5:25), letting strife alone before it is meddled with, or when it is meddled with, seeking to end it as quickly as may be, as in the sight of God.

A Neighbor

Next, the peacemaker is a neighbor, and he never seeks to meddle with his neighbor's disputes, especially if it is a dispute between his neighbor and his neighbor's wife, for he knows well that if they disagree, they will both agree very soon to disagree with him if he meddles between them. If he is called in when there is a dispute between two neighbors, he never excites them to animosity, but he says to them, "You do not do well; why do you strive with one other?" Although he does not take the wrong side, but always seeks to do justice, he always tempers his justice with mercy and says to the one who is wronged, "Can you not have the nobility to forgive?" And he sometimes puts himself between the two, when they are very angry, and takes the blows from both sides, for he knows that the same was done by Jesus, who took the blows from His Father and from us also, so that by suffering in our stead, peace might be made between God and man.

The peacemaker acts in this way whenever he is called to do his good offices, and more especially if his station enables him to do it with authority. He endeavors, if he sits upon the judgment seat, not to bring a case to a trial, if it can be arranged otherwise. If he is a minister and there is a difference among his people, he does not enter into the details, for he knows well that there is much idle gossip. Instead, he says, "Peace" to the billows, and "Hush" to the winds, and so he bids men live. He thinks that they have such a short time to dwell together, it is proper that they should live in harmony. And so he says, *"How pleasant it is for brethren to dwell together in unity!"* (Ps. 133:1).

A Christian

"Christian" is the peacemaker's highest title. Being a Christian, he unites himself with a Christian church, and here, as a peacemaker, he is as an angel of God. Even among churches there are those who are bowed down with infirmities, and these infirmities cause Christian men and Christian women to differ at times. So the peacemaker says, "This is improper, my brother; let us be at peace." He remembers what Paul said, *"I beseech Euodias, and beseech Syntyche, that they be of the same mind in the Lord"* (Phil. 4:2). He thinks that if these two were thus besought by Paul to be of the same mind, unity must be a blessed thing, and he labors for it.

Sometimes the peacemaker, when he sees differences likely to arise between his denomination and others, turns to the history of Abram. He reads how the herdsmen of Abram had a strife with the herdsman of Lot, and he notes that in the same verse it is said, *"And the Canaanite and the Perizzite dwelled then in the land"* (Gen. 13:7). So he thinks it was a shame that where there were Perizzites to look on, followers of the true God should disagree. He says to Christians, "Do not do this, for we make the Devil sport, we dishonor God, we damage our own cause, and we ruin the souls of men." And he says, "Put your swords into your scabbards, be at peace, and do not fight with one another." They who are not peacemakers, when received into a church, will fight about the smallest whim and will differ about the minutest point. I have known churches torn in pieces and schisms committed in Christian bodies, through things so foolish that a wise man could not understand the reason; through things so ridiculous that a reasonable man must have overlooked them.

The peacemaker says, *"Follow peace with all men"* (Heb. 12:14). He prays especially that the Spirit of God, who is the Spirit of Peace, might rest upon the church at all times, binding believers together in one. Believers then being one in Christ, the world may know that the Father has sent His Son into the world, heralded as His mission was with an angelic song: *"Glory to God in the highest, and on earth peace, good will toward men"* (Luke 2:14).

Now, I trust in the description that I have given of the peacemaker, I may have described some of you who are reading this, but I fear most would have to say, "Well, in many things I fall short." Two Spartans had quarreled with each other, and the Spartan king, Aris, bade them both meet him in a temple. When they were both there, he heard their differences, and he said to the priest, "Lock the doors of the temple; these two will never go forth until they get along." There, within the temple, he said, "It is not proper to differ." So they settled their differences at once and went away. If this were done in an idol temple, much more let it be done in the house of God. If the Spartan heathen did this, much more let the Christian, the believer in Christ, do it. This very day, put aside all bitterness and all malice from you, and say one to another, "If in anything you have offended me, it is forgiven, and if in anything I have offended you, I confess my error. Let the breach be healed, and as the children of God, let us be in union with one another." Blessed are they who can do this for *"blessed are the peacemakers!"*

THE PEACEMAKER'S BLESSEDNESS

Blessed by God

I know that he whom God blesses is blessed, and he whom God curses is cursed. God blesses him from the highest heavens; God blesses him in a godlike manner; God blesses him with the abundant blessings that are treasured up in Christ.

While the peacemaker is blessed by God, the blessedness is diffused through his own soul. His conscience bears witness that he has sought to honor Christ among men as in the sight of God through the Holy Spirit. More especially, he is most blessed when he has been most assailed with curses, for then the assurance greets him, *"so persecuted they the prophets which were before you"* (Matt. 5:12). And whereas he has a command to rejoice at all times, yet he finds a special command to be exceedingly glad when he is ill-treated. Therefore, he takes it well, if for well-doing he is called to suffer, and he rejoices to bear a part of the Savior's cross in this way. He goes to his bed—no dreams of enmity disturb his sleep. He rises and goes about his business, and he does not fear the face of any man, for he can say, "I do not have anything in my heart but friendship toward all"; or if he is attacked with slander, and his enemies have forged a lie against him, he can nevertheless say,

> He that forged, and he that threw the dart,
> Has each a brother's interest in my heart.

Loving all, he is then peaceful in his own soul, and he is blessed as one who inherits the blessing of the Most High.

Frequently, it comes to pass that he is even blessed by the wicked, for though they want to withhold a good word from him, they cannot. Overcoming evil with good, he heaps coals of fire upon their heads (Rom. 12:20) and melts the coldness of their enmity, until even they say, "He is a good man." And when he dies, those whom he has helped to be at peace with one another say over his grave, "It would be good if the world would see many like him; there would not be half the strife or half the sin in it, if there were many like him."

One of the Children of God

He is a child of God by adoption and grace, but peacemaking is a sweet evidence of the work of the peaceful Spirit within. As the child of God, moreover, he has a likeness to his Father who is in heaven. God is peaceful, long-suffering, and tender, full of loving-kindness, pity, and compassion. So, too, is this peacemaker. Being like God, he bears his Father's image. In this way he testifies to men that he is one of God's children. As one of God's children, the peacemaker has access to his Father. He goes to Him with confidence, saying, *"Our Father which art in heaven"* (Matt. 6:9), which he dare not say unless he could plead with a clear conscience, *"Forgive us our debts, as we forgive our debtors"* (v. 12). He feels the tie of brotherhood with man, and therefore he feels that he may rejoice in the fatherhood of God. He comes with confidence and with intense delight to his Father who is in heaven, for he is one of the children of the Highest, who does good both to the unthankful and to the evil.

Called a Child of God

"They shall be called the children of God." They not only are so, but they will be called so. That is, even their enemies will call them so. Even the world will say, "That man is a child of God." Perhaps, beloved, there is nothing that so strikes the ungodly as the peaceful behavior of a Christian under insult.

There was a soldier in India, a big fellow who had been, before he enlisted, a prizefighter and afterwards had performed many deeds of valor. When he had been converted through the preaching of a missionary, all his fellow soldiers made a laughingstock of him. They counted it impossible that such a man as he had been would become a peaceful Christian. So one day when they were at dinner, one of them flagrantly threw into his face and chest a whole bowlful of scalding soup. The poor man tore his clothes open to wipe away the scalding liquid, and yet self-possessed amid his excitement, he said, "I am a Christian; I must expect this," and smiled at them.

The one who did it said, "If I had thought you would have taken it that way, I would never have done it; I am very sorry I ever did so." His patience rebuked their malice, and they all said he was a Christian. Thus, he was called a child of God. They saw in him an evidence that was to them all the more striking, because they knew that they could not have done the same.

When Mr. Kilpin, of Exeter, was walking along the streets one day, an evil man pushed him from the pavement into the gutter, and as he fell into the gutter, the man said, "Lay there, John Bunyan; that is good enough for you." Mr. Kilpin got up and went on his way, and afterwards, when this man wanted to know how he took the insult, he was surprised that all Mr. Kilpin said was that he had done him more honor than dishonor, for he thought that being called John Bunyan was worth being rolled in the gutter a thousand times. Then he who had done this said that Mr. Kilpin was a good man.

So, they who are peacemakers are *"called the children of God."* They demonstrate to the world in such a way that the very blind must see and the very deaf must hear that God is in them. Oh, that we had enough grace to win this blessed commendation! If God has brought you far enough, my reader, to hunger and thirst for righteousness, I pray you never cease your hunger until He has brought you so far as to be a peacemaker, in order that you may be called a child of God.

THE PEACEMAKER AT WORK

You have much work to do, I do not doubt, in your own households and your own circles of acquaintance. Go and do it. You remember well that text in Job, *"Can that which is unsavoury be eaten without salt? or is there any taste in the white of an egg?"* (Job 6:6), by which Job wants us to know that unsavory things must have something else with them or else they will not be pleasant for food. Now, our religion is an unsavory thing to men. We must put salt with it, and this salt must be our quietness and peacemaking disposition. Then, they who would have shunned our religion when it stood alone will say of it, when they see the salt with it, "This is good," and they will find some relish in this "white of an egg."

You should commend your godliness to the sons of men, and in your own houses make clear and clean work, purging out the old leaven, so that you may offer sacrifices to God of a godly and heavenly sort. If you have any conflicts among you or any divisions, I pray you, even as God, for Christ's sake, forgave you, so also should you forgive (Eph. 4:32). By the bloody sweat of Him who prayed for you, and by the agonies of Him who died for you and in dying said, *"Father, forgive them; for they know not what they do"* (Luke 23:34), forgive your enemies; *"bless them that curse you...and pray for them which despitefully use you"* (Matt. 5:44). Let it be always said of you, as a Christian, "That man is meek and lowly in heart, and would sooner bear injury himself than cause an injury to another."

However, the chief work I want you to take up is this: the work of Jesus Christ, who was the greatest of all peacemakers. *"He is our peace"* (Eph. 2:14). He came to make peace with Jew and Gentile, *"for he...hath made both one, and hath broken down the middle wall of partition between us"* (v. 14). He came to make peace between all striving nationalities, for we are *"neither Greek...Barbarian, Scythian, bond nor free: but Christ is all, and in all"* (Col. 3:11). He came to make peace between His Father's justice and our offending souls, and He has made peace for us through the blood of His cross.

Now, you who are the sons of peace, endeavor as instruments in His hands to make peace between God and men. Let your earnest prayers go up to heaven for your children's souls. Let your supplications never cease for the souls of all your acquaintance and kinsfolk. Pray for the salvation of your perishing fellow creatures. In this way you will be peacemakers. And when you have prayed, use all the means within your power. Preach if God has given you the ability; preach with the Holy Spirit sent down from heaven—the reconciling Word of life. Teach, if you cannot preach. Teach the Word. *"Be instant in season, out of season"* (2 Tim. 4:2). *"Sow beside all waters"* (Isa. 32:20), for the Gospel *"speaketh better things than* [the blood] *of Abel"* (Heb. 12:24) and cries peace to the sons of men. Write to your friends about Christ, and if you cannot speak much, speak a little for Him. But, oh, make it the object of your life to win others for Christ.

Never be satisfied with going to heaven alone. Ask the Lord that you may be the spiritual father of many children and that God may bless you to the gathering in of much of the Redeemer's harvest. I thank God that there are so many Christians who are alive to the love of souls. It makes my heart glad to hear of conversions and to receive the converts, but I feel most glad when converts are made the means of the conversion of others. Blessed are such peacemakers! You have saved a soul from death and hidden a multitude of sins (James 5:20). *"They that turn many to righteousness* [will shine] *as the stars for ever and ever"* (Dan. 12:3). They, indeed, in heaven itself *"shall be called the children of God."* The genealogy of that book, in which the names of all the Lord's people are written, will record that through God the Holy Spirit they have brought souls into the bond of peace through Jesus Christ.

ENDEAVORING TO BE A PEACEMAKER

This chapter speaks to many people who know nothing of peace, for *"there is no peace, saith my God, to the wicked"* (Isa. 57:21). *"The wicked are like the troubled sea, when it cannot rest, whose waters cast up mire and dirt"* (v. 20). I do not address this to you with any desire of making a false peace with your souls. Woe to the prophets who say, *"Peace, peace; when there is no peace"* (Jer. 6:14). Rather let me, first of all, expose the warring state of your soul that is without peace.

O soul! You are at war with your conscience. You have tried to quiet it, but it will prick you. You have shut up the recorder of the town of Mansoul in a dark place, as in Bunyan's *The Pilgrim's Progress,* and you have built a wall before his door. Still, when he has his fits, your conscience will thunder at you and say, "This is not right; this is the path that leads to hell; this is the road of destruction."

Oh, there are some of you to whom conscience is like a ghost, haunting you by day and night. You know the good, though you choose the evil. You prick your fingers with the thorns of conscience when you

172

try to pluck the rose of sin. To you the downward path is not an easy one; it is hedged up and ditched up. There are many bars and gates and chains on this road, but you climb over them, determined to ruin your own souls.

Oh, there is war between you and conscience. Conscience says, "Turn," but you say, "I will not." Conscience says, "Close your shop on Sunday." Conscience says, "Alter this system of trade; it is cheating." Conscience says, "Stop drinking that alcohol; it makes the man into something worse than a brute." Conscience says, "Rip yourself from that unchaste connection; be done with that evil; bolt your door against lust," but you say, "I will drink the sweet, even though it damns me. I will still go to my haunts, though I perish in my sins."

There is war between you and your conscience. Your conscience is God's deputy in your soul. Let conscience speak a moment or two right now. Do not fear him; he is a good friend to you. Though he speaks roughly, the day will come when you will know that there is more music in the very roarings of conscience than in all the sweet and enticing tones that lust adopts to cheat you to your ruin. Let your conscience speak.

Moreover, there is war between you and God's law. The Ten Commandments are against you. The first one comes forward and says, "Let him be cursed, for he denies Me. He has another God besides me. His God is his belly; he yields homage to his lust." All the Ten Commandments, like ten great cannons, are pointed at you today, for you have broken all God's statutes and lived in the daily neglect of all His commands.

God Will Bless You

Soul! You will find it a hard thing to go to war with the Law. When the Law came in peace, Sinai was completely in smoke, and even Moses said, *"I exceedingly fear and quake"* (Heb. 12:21). What will you do when the Law comes in terror, when the trumpet of the archangel will tear you from your grave, when the eyes of God will burn their way into your guilty soul, when the great books will be opened, and all your sin and shame will be punished? Can you stand against an angry Law in that day? When the officers of the Law will come forth to deliver you up to the tormentors and cast you away forever from peace and happiness, sinner, what will you do? Can you dwell with everlasting fire? Can you abide the eternal burning? Oh,

Agree with thine adversary quickly, whiles thou art in the way with him; lest at any time the adversary deliver thee to the judge, and the judge deliver thee to the officer, and thou be cast into prison. Verily I say unto thee, Thou shalt by no means come out thence, till thou hast paid the uttermost farthing. (Matt. 5:25-26)

But, sinner, do you know that you are right now at war with God? You have forgotten and neglected the Lord who made you and is your best friend. He has fed you, and you have used your strength against Him. He has clothed you—the clothes you have upon your back today are the garb of His goodness—yet, instead of being the servant of Him whose garments you wear, you are the slave of His greatest enemy. The very breath in your nostrils is the loan of His charity, and yet you use that breath perhaps to curse Him or at the best, in lewdness or loose conversation, to do dishonor to His laws. He who made you has become your enemy through your sin, and today you are still hating Him and despising His Word.

You say, "I do not hate Him." Soul, I charge you then, "Believe in the Lord Jesus Christ." "No," you say, "I cannot, I will not do that!" Then you hate Him. If you loved Him, you would keep His great command. *"His commandments are not grievous"* (1 John 5:3); they are sweet and easy. You would believe in His Son if you did love the Father, for *"every one that loveth* [the Father] *loveth him also that is begotten of him"* (1 John 5:1).

Are you at war with God in this way? Surely this is a sorry plight for you to be in. Can you meet Him who comes against you with ten thousand? Can you stand against Him who is almighty, who makes heaven shake at His reproof and breaks the crooked serpent with a word? Do you hope to hide from Him? *"Can any hide himself in secret places that I shall not see him? saith the LORD"* (Jer. 23:24). Even though you dive into the caverns of the sea, He will there command the crooked serpent, and it will bite you. If you make your bed in hell, He will find you out; if you climb to heaven, He is there (Ps. 139:8). Creation is your prison house, and He can find you when He will. Or do you think you can endure His fury? Are your ribs of iron? Are you bones brass? If they are so, they will melt like wax before the coming of the Lord God of hosts, for He is mighty, and as a lion He will tear His prey in pieces, and as a fire He will devour His adversary, *"for our God is a consuming fire"* (Heb. 12:29).

This, then, is the state of every unconverted man and woman. You are at war with conscience, at war with God's law, and at war with God Himself. And, now, then, as God's ambassadors, we come to talk of peace. I urge you to give heed. *"As though God did beseech you by* [me, I] *pray you in Christ's stead, be ye reconciled to God"* (2 Cor. 5:20). I am imploring you, *"in Christ's stead."*

Look and listen. It is Christ speaking to you now. I think I hear Him speak to some of you. This is the way He speaks: "Soul, I love you; I love you from My heart. I would not have you at enmity with My Father." The tears prove the truth of what He states, while He cries, *"How often would I have gathered* [you], *even as a hen gathereth her chickens under her wings, and ye would not!"* (Matt. 23:37). "Yet," He says, "I come to treat you with peace. *'Come now, and let us reason together'* (Isa. 1:18). *'I will make an everlasting covenant with you, even the sure mercies of David'* (Isa. 55:3)". "Sinner," He says, "you are guilty and condemned; will you confess this? Are you willing to throw down your weapons now and say, Almighty God, I yield, I yield; I would no longer be Your foe?" If so, peace is proclaimed to you. *"Let the wicked forsake his way, and the unrighteous man his thoughts: and let him return unto the* LORD, *and he will have mercy upon him; and to our God, for he will abundantly pardon"* (v. 7). Pardon is freely presented to every soul who sincerely repents of his sin, but that pardon must come to you through faith.

So Jesus stands here, points to the wounds upon His breast, and spreads His bleeding hands. He says, "Sinner, trust in Me and live!" God no longer proclaims to you His fiery law, but His sweet, His simple Gospel, which is "believe and live." *"He that believeth on* [the Son] *is not condemned: but he that believeth not is condemned already, because he hath not believed in the name of the only begotten Son of God"* (John 3:18). *"As Moses lifted up the serpent in the wilderness, even so must the Son of man be lifted up: that whosoever believeth in him should not perish, but have eternal life"* (vv. 14–15).

O soul, does the Spirit of God move in you now? Do you say, "Lord, I would be at peace with you"? Are you willing to take Christ on His own terms in the matter, and give yourself up, body, soul, and spirit, to be saved by Him? Now, if my Master were visibly in front of you, I think He would plead with you in such a way that you would say, "Lord, I believe; I want to be at peace with you." But even Christ Himself never converted a soul apart from the Holy Spirit, and even as a preacher, He did not win many to Him, for they were hard of heart. If the Holy Spirit is present as you are reading this, He may as much bless you when I plead in Christ's stead as though He pleaded Himself.

Soul! Will you have Christ or not? Young men, young women, you may never hear about this Word again. Will you die at enmity against God? You who are sitting there, still unconverted, you may never see tomorrow. Would you go into eternity, *"enemies* [to God]...*by wicked works"* (Col. 1:21)? Soul! Will you have Christ or not? Say, "No," if you mean it. Say, "No, Christ, I will never be saved by You." Say it. Look the matter in the face. But I pray that you do not say, "I will give no answer." Come, give some answer this very moment—yes, this very moment. Thank God you can give an answer. Thank God you are not in hell. Thank God that your sentence has not been pronounced, that you have not received what you have deserved. God help you to give the right answer!

Will you have Christ or not? "I am not fit." There is no question of fitness; it is, will you have Him? "My heart is black." He will come into your black heart and clean it. "Oh, but I am hard-hearted." He will come into your hard heart and soften it. Will you have Him? You can have Him if you will. When God makes a soul willing, it is a clear proof that He means to give Christ to that soul, and if you are willing, He is not unwilling. If He has made you willing, you may have Him. "Oh," says one, "I cannot think that I might have Christ." Soul, you may have Him now. Mary, He calls you! John, he calls you! Sinner, whoever you may be reading this, if there is a holy willingness toward Christ in your soul, or if there is even a faint desire toward Him, He calls you, He calls you! Oh, do not tarry, but come and trust in Him.

Oh, if I had such a Gospel as this to preach to lost souls in hell, what an effect it would have upon them! Surely, surely, if they could once more have the Gospel preached in their ears, I think the tears would wet their poor cheeks, and they would say, "Almighty God, if we may but escape from Your wrath, we will lay hold on Christ." But sometimes the Gospel is preached in your church, preached every day, until I fear you listen to it as an old, old story. Perhaps it is the pastor's poor way of telling it, but God knows, if we knew how to tell it better, we would do so. O my Master, send better ambassadors to people, if that will woo them. Send more earnest pleaders, and more tender hearts, if that will bring them to Yourself! But, oh, bring them, bring them! Our hearts long to see them brought.

Sinner, will you have Christ or not? Now is the time of God's power to some of your souls, I know. The Holy Spirit is striving with some of you. Lord, win them, conquer them, overcome them! Do you say, "Yes, happy day! I want to be led in triumph, captive to my Lord's great love"? Soul, it is done, if you believe. Trust Christ, and your many sins are all forgiven you. Cast yourself before His dear cross, and say,

> A guilty, weak, and helpless worm,
>   Into Thy arms I fall;
> Be Thou my strength and righteousness,
>   My Jesus and my all.

And if He rejects or refuses you, tell of it. There was never such a case yet. He always has received those who come. He always will. He is an openhanded and an openhearted Savior.

O sinner, may God bring you to put your trust in Him once for all! Spirits above, tune your harps anew. There is a sinner born to God right now. Lead the song, O Saul of Tarsus! And follow the sinner with sweetest music, O Mary! Let music roll up before the throne today, for it is there that heirs of glory are born and prodigals have returned! To God be the glory forever and ever! Amen.

Appendix

An Exposition of Scripture: The Beatitudes and Beyond

MATTHEW 5:1–6:4

5:1–2 *And seeing the multitudes, he went up into a mountain: and when he was set, his disciples came unto him: and he opened his mouth, and taught them, saying...*

Our Savior soon gathered a congregation. The multitudes perceived in Him a love for them and a willingness to impart blessing to them, and therefore they gathered about Him. He chose the mountain and the open air for the delivery of this great discourse. He went there for convenience and quietude, and to be out of the way of traffic. Elevated doctrines would seem most at home on the high places of the earth.

"And when he was set." The Preacher sat, and the people stood. This was the mode of Eastern teaching. We might make a helpful change if we were sometimes to adopt a similar plan now. I am afraid that ease of posture may contribute to the creation of slumber of heart in many hearers. There, Christ sat, and *"his disciples came unto him."* They formed the inner circle that was the nearest to Him, and He imparted to them His choicest secrets.

He also spoke to the multitude, and therefore it is said that *"he opened his mouth,"* as well He might when there were such great truths to proceed from it, and so vast a crowd to hear them. Chrysostom says that He taught them even when He did not open his mouth; His very silence was instructive. But when He did open His mouth, what streams of wisdom flowed forth! He *"taught them."* He did not open His mouth to make an oration. He was a Teacher, so His aim was to teach those who came to Him. *"He opened his mouth, and taught them, saying..."*

5:3 *Blessed are the poor in spirit: for theirs is the kingdom of heaven.*

This is a gracious beginning to our Savior's discourse: *"Blessed are the poor."* The Old Testament closes with the word *"curse"* (Mal. 4:6). The New Testament begins here, in the preaching of Christ, with the word *"Blessed."* He has changed the curse into a blessing: *"Blessed."*

No one ever considered the poor as Jesus did, but here He is speaking of a poverty of spirit, a lowliness of heart, an absence of self-esteem. Where that kind of spirit is found, it is sweet poverty: *"Blessed are the poor in spirit: for theirs is the kingdom of heaven."* It is a paradox that puzzles many, for the poor in spirit often seem to have nothing; yet they have the kingdom of heaven, so they have everything. He who thinks the least of himself is the man of whom God thinks the most. You are not poor in God's sight if you are poor in spirit.

5:4 *Blessed are they that mourn: for they shall be comforted.*

There is a blessing that often goes with mourning itself, but when the sorrow is of a spiritual sort—mourning for sin—then is it blessed indeed.

They are not only poor in spirit, but they are weeping, lamenting, mourning. People of the world are frivolous, frolicsome, lighthearted, and loving everything that is akin to mirth; yet it is not said of them, but of those who mourn, that *"they shall be comforted."*

5:5a *Blessed are the meek...*

The meek are the quiet-spirited, the gentle, the self-sacrificing; not your high-spirited, quick-tempered men who will put up with no insult, your bullying, lofty ones who are always ready to resent any real or imagined disrespect—there is nothing here for them. But blessed are the gentle, those who are ready to be thought nothing of.

5:5b *For they shall inherit the earth.*

It looks as if they would be pushed out of the world, but they will not be, *"for they shall inherit the earth."* The wolves devour the sheep, yet there are more sheep in the world than there are wolves, and the sheep continue to multiply and to feed in green pastures.

Some say that the best way to get through the world is to swagger along with a coarse impudence and to push out of your way all who may be in it. But there is no truth in this idea. The truth lies in quite another direction: *"Blessed are the meek: for they shall inherit the earth."*

5:6 *Blessed are they which do hunger and thirst after righteousness: for they shall be filled.*

Pining to be holy, longing to serve God, eager to spread every righteous principle—blessed are they. The course of these Beatitudes is like descending stairs. They began with spiritual poverty, went on to mourning, came down to gentle-spiritedness, and now we come to hunger and thirst. Yet, we have been going up all the time, for here we read, *"They shall be filled."* What more can we have than full satisfaction?

5:7 *Blessed are the merciful: for they shall obtain mercy.*

Those who are kind, generous, sympathetic, ready to forgive those who have wronged them— blessed are they. *"The merciful"* are those who are always ready to forgive, always ready to help the poor and needy, always ready to overlook what they might well condemn, and *"they shall obtain mercy."*

5:8a *Blessed are the pure in heart...*

It is a most blessed attainment to have such a longing for purity as to love everything that is chaste and holy and to abhor everything that is questionable and unhallowed.

5:8b *For they shall see God.*

There is a wonderful connection between hearts and eyes. A man who has the stains of filth on his soul cannot see God, but they who are purified in heart are purified in vision too: *"they shall see God."* When the heart is washed, the dirt is taken from the mental eye. The heart that loves God is connected with an understanding that perceives God. There is no way of seeing God until the heart is renewed by sovereign grace. It is not greatness of intellect, but purity of affection that enables us to see God.

5:9 *Blessed are the peacemakers: for they shall be called the children of God.*

They are those who always end a quarrel if they can, those who put themselves out to prevent discord. They are not only the passively peaceful, but the actively peaceful, who try to rectify mistakes and to end all quarrels in a peaceful way. They will not only be the children of God, but men will call them so; others will recognize in them their likeness to the peacemaking God.

5:10 *Blessed are they which are persecuted for righteousness' sake: for theirs is the kingdom of heaven.*

They share the kingdom of heaven with the poor in spirit. They often have evil spoken of them. They sometimes have to suffer the spoiling of their goods—many of them have laid down their lives for Christ's sake—but they are truly blessed, for *"theirs is the kingdom of heaven."* They have it now. They are participating in it already, for, as Christ was persecuted and He is again persecuted in them, since they are partakers of His sufferings, so they are also sharers in His kingdom.

5:11 *Blessed are ye, when men shall revile you, and persecute you, and shall say all manner of evil against you falsely, for my sake.*

Be aware that it must be said falsely, and it must be for Christ's sake, if you are to be blessed. There is no blessing in having evil spoken of you truthfully, or in having it spoken of you falsely because of some bitterness in your own spirit.

5:12 *Rejoice, and be exceeding glad: for great is your reward in heaven: for so persecuted they the prophets which were before you.*

If you cheerfully bear reproach of this kind for Christ's sake, you are in the true prophetic succession. You prove that you have the stamp and seal of those who are in the service of God. You have an elevation by persecution; you are lifted into the peerage of martyrdom; though you occupy only an inferior place in it, you are still in it. Therefore, *"rejoice, and be exceeding glad."*

5:13a *Ye are the salt of the earth...*

Followers of Christ, *"ye are the salt of the earth."* You help to preserve it and to subdue the corruption that is in it.

5:13b *But if the salt have lost his savour, wherewith shall it be salted?*

A professing Christian with no grace in him—a religious man whose very religion is dead—what is the good of him? And he is himself in a hopeless condition. You can salt meat, but you cannot salt salt.

5:13c *It is thenceforth good for nothing, but to be cast out, and to be trodden under foot of men.*

There are people who believe that you can be children of God today and children of the Devil tomorrow, then children of God again the next day and children of the Devil again the day after. But, believe me, it is not so. If the work of grace is really worked by God in your soul, it will last throughout your whole life, and if it does not last, that proves that it is not the work of God. God does not put His hand to this work a second time. There is no regeneration twice over; you can be born again, but you cannot be born again and again and again as some teach. There is no note in Scripture of that kind. Therefore, I do rejoice that regeneration, once truly worked by the Spirit of God, is an incorruptible seed that lives and abides forever (1 Pet. 1:23). But beware, professing Christian, in case you should be like salt that has lost its savor, and that is therefore good for nothing.

5:14 *Ye are the light of the world. A city that is set on an hill cannot be hid.*

Christ never contemplated producing secret Christians—Christians whose virtues would never be displayed—pilgrims who would travel to heaven by night and never be seen by their fellow pilgrims or anyone else.

5:15 *Neither do men light a candle, and put it under a bushel, but on a candlestick; and it giveth light unto all that are in the house.*

Christians ought to be seen, and they ought to let their light be seen. They should never even attempt to conceal it. If you are a lamp, you have no right to be under a bushel or under a bed. Your place is on the lamp stand where your light can be seen.

5:16 *Let your light so shine before men, that they may see your good works, and glorify your Father which is in heaven.*

Not that they may glorify you, but that they may glorify your Father who is in heaven.

5:17–18 *Think not that I am come to destroy the law, or the prophets: I am not come to destroy, but to fulfil. For verily I say unto you, Till heaven and earth pass, one jot or one tittle shall in no wise pass from the law, till all be fulfilled.*

No cross of a "t" and no dot of an "i" will be taken from God's law. Its requirements will always be the same, immutably fixed, and never to be abated by so little as *"one jot or one tittle."*

5:19–20a *Whosoever therefore shall break one of these least commandments, and shall teach men so,* *he shall be called the least in the kingdom of heaven: but whosoever shall do and teach them, the same shall be called great in the kingdom of heaven. For I say unto you, That except your righteousness shall exceed the righteousness of the scribes and Pharisees...*

The Pharisees seemed to have reached the very highest degree of righteousness. Indeed, they themselves thought they went rather over the mark than under it, but Christ says to His disciples, "Unless your righteousness goes beyond that..."

5:20b *Ye shall in no case enter into the kingdom of heaven.*

These are solemn words of warning. God grant that we may have a righteousness that exceeds that of the scribes and Pharisees, a righteousness worked in us by the Spirit of God, a righteousness of the heart and of the life!

5:21 *Ye have heard that it was said by them of old time, Thou shalt not kill; and whosoever shall kill shall be in danger of the judgment.*

Antiquity is often pleaded as an authority, but our King makes short work of *"them of old time."* He begins with one of their alterations of His Father's law. They added to the sacred oracles. The first part of the saying that our Lord quoted was divine, but it was dragged down to a low level by the addition about the human court and the murderer's liability to appear there. In this way, it became a proverb among men rather than an inspired utterance from the mouth of God. Its meaning, as God spoke it, had a far wider range than when the offense was restrained to actual killing, such as could be brought before a human judgment seat. To narrow a command is to annul it measurably. We may not do this even with antiquity for our basis. The whole truth newly stated is better than an old falsehood in ancient language.

5:22 *But I say unto you, That whosoever is angry with his brother without a cause shall be in danger of the judgment: and whosoever shall say to his brother, Raca, shall be in danger of the council: but whosoever shall say, Thou fool, shall be in danger of hell fire.*

Murder lies within anger, for we wish harm to the object of our wrath or even wish that he did not exist, and this is to kill him in the desire. Anger *"without a cause"* is forbidden by the command that says, *"Thou shalt not kill"* (v. 21), for unjust anger is like premeditated murder. Such anger without cause brings us under higher judgment than that of Jewish law courts. God takes notice of the emotions from which acts of hate may spring and calls us to account as much for the angry feeling as for the murderous deed.

Words also come under the same condemnation: a man will be judged for what he *"shall say to his brother."* To call a man *"Raca,"* or a worthless fellow, is to kill him in his reputation, and to say to him, *"Thou fool,"* is to kill him by denying that he possesses the noblest characteristics of a man. Therefore, all this comes under such censure as men

190

distribute in their councils, but more than this, and under what is far worse, the punishment awarded by the highest court of the universe, which dooms men to *"hell fire."* Thus our Lord and King restores the law of God to its true force and warns us that it denounces not only the overt act of killing, but every thought, feeling, and word that would tend to injure a brother or annihilate him by contempt.

5:23–24 *Therefore if thou bring thy gift to the altar, and there rememberest that thy brother hath ought against thee; leave there thy gift before the altar, and go thy way; first be reconciled to thy brother, and then come and offer thy gift.*

The Pharisee, as a cover for his malice, would bring a sacrifice to make atonement, but our Lord wants us to render forgiveness to our brothers first and then present the offering. We ought to worship God thoughtfully, and if in the course of that thought we remember that our brothers have anything against us, we must stop. If we have wronged another, we are to pause, cease from our worship, and hasten to seek reconciliation. We easily remember if we have anything against our brothers, but now the memory is to be turned the other way. Only when we have remembered our wrongdoing and have made reconciliation can we hope for acceptance with the Lord. The rule is: first, peace with man, and then, acceptance with God. The holy must be traversed to reach the Holiest of All. Peace having been made with our brothers, then let us conclude our service toward our Father, and we will do so with lighter hearts and truer zeal.

I would anxiously desire to be at peace with all men before I attempt to worship God, for fear that I present the sacrifice of fools to God.

5:25–26 *Agree with thine adversary quickly, whiles thou art in the way with him; lest at any time the adversary deliver thee to the judge, and the judge deliver thee to the officer, and thou be cast into prison. Verily I say unto thee, Thou shalt by no means come out thence, till thou hast paid the uttermost farthing.*

Be eager for peace in all disagreements. Stop strife before you begin. In lawsuits, seek speedy and peaceful settlements. Often, in our Lord's days, this was the most profitable way, and usually it is so now. It is better to lose your rights than to get into the hands of those who will only fleece you in the name of justice and hold you fast, as long as a semblance of a demand can stand against you or another penny can be extracted from you. In a country where "justice" meant robbery, it was wisdom to be robbed and to make no complaint. Even in our own country, a lean settlement is better than a fat lawsuit. Many go into the court to get wool, but come out closely shorn. Carry on no angry suits in courts, but make peace with the utmost promptness.

5:27–28 *Ye have heard that it was said by them of old time, Thou shalt not commit adultery: but I say unto you, That whosoever looketh on a woman to lust after her hath committed adultery with her already in his heart.*

In this case our King again sets aside how men have glossed over the commands of God and makes the law to be seen in its vast spiritual breadth. Whereas tradition had confined the prohibition to an overt act, the King shows that it forbade the unclean desires of the heart. Here the divine law is shown to refer, not only to the act of criminal behavior, but even to the desire, imagination, or passion that would suggest such an infamy. What a King we have, who stretches His scepter over the realm of our inward lusts! How sovereignly He puts it: *"But I say unto you"*! Who but a divine being has authority to speak in this fashion? His word is law. And so it ought to be, seeing that He touches vice at the fountainhead and forbids uncleanness in the heart. If sin were not allowed in the mind, it would never be made manifest in the body; this, therefore, is a very effective way of dealing with the evil. But how searching, how condemning! Irregular looks, unchaste desires, and strong passions are of the very essence of adultery, and who can claim a lifelong freedom from them? Yet these are the things that defile a man. Lord, purge them out of my nature, and make me pure within!

5:29 *And if thy right eye offend thee, pluck it out, and cast it from thee: for it is profitable for thee that one of thy members should perish, and not that thy whole body should be cast into hell.*

That which is the cause of sin is to be given up as well as the sin itself. It is not sinful to have an eye or to cultivate keen perception, but if the eye of speculative knowledge leads us to offend by intellectual sin, it becomes the cause of evil and must be mortified. I am to get rid of anything, however harmless, that leads me to do or think or feel wrongly, as much as if it were in itself an evil. Though it would involve deprivation to get rid of it, it must be dispensed with, since even a serious loss in one direction is far better than the losing of the whole man. To be a blind saint is far better than a quick-sighted sinner. If abstaining from alcohol caused weakness of body, it would be better to be weak than to be strong and fall into drunkenness. Since vain speculation and reasoning land men in unbelief, we will have none of them. To *"be cast into hell"* is too great a risk to run, merely to indulge the evil eye of lust or curiosity.

5:30 *And if thy right hand offend thee, cut it off, and cast it from thee: for it is profitable for thee that one of thy members should perish, and not that thy whole body should be cast into hell.*

The cause of offense may be active like the hand instead of intellectual like the eye, but it would be better to be hindered in our work than to be drawn aside into temptation. The most dexterous hand must not be spared if it encourages us in doing evil. It is not because a certain thing may make us clever and successful that therefore we are to allow it. If it should prove to be the frequent cause of our falling into sin, we must be done with it and place ourselves at a disadvantage for our lifework, rather than ruin our whole being by sin. Holiness is to be our first object; everything else must take a very secondary place. Right eyes and right hands are no longer right if they lead us wrongly. Even hands and eyes must go so that we may not offend our God by them. Yet,

let no man read this literally and therefore mutilate
his body, as some foolish fanatics have done. The
real meaning is clear enough.

5:31–32 *It hath been said, Whosoever shall put away
his wife, let him give her a writing of divorcement:
but I say unto you, That whosoever shall put away
his wife, saving for the cause of fornication, causeth
her to commit adultery: and whosoever shall marry
her that is divorced committeth adultery.*

This time our King quotes and condemns a per-
missive law of the Jewish state. Men were accustomed
to bidding their wives "begone," and a hasty word was
thought sufficient as an act of divorce. Moses insisted
upon *"a writing of divorcement,"* so that angry passions might have time to cool and that the separation,
if it must come, might be performed with deliberation
and legal formality. The requirement of a writing was
to a certain degree a check upon an evil habit, which
was so ingrained in the people that to refuse it altogether would have been useless and would only have
created another crime. The law of Moses went as far
as it could practically be enforced. It was because of
the hardness of their hearts that divorce was tolerated; it was never approved.

However, our Lord was more heroic in His legislation. He forbade divorce except for the one crime
of infidelity to the marriage vow. Anyone who com-
mits adultery does by that act and deed in effect
break the marriage bond, and it ought then to be
formally recognized by the state as being broken.
For nothing else should a man be divorced from his
wife. Marriage is for life and cannot be loosed, except

by the one great crime which severs its bond, whichever of the two is guilty of it. Our Lord would never have tolerated the wicked laws of the United States that allow married men and women to separate on the merest pretext. A woman who divorces for any cause but adultery and marries again is committing adultery before God, whatever the laws of man may call it. This is very plain and positive, and thus a sanctity is given to marriage that human legislation ought not to violate.

Let us not be among those who take up novel ideas of wedlock and seek to deform the marriage laws under the pretense of reforming them. Our Lord knows better than our modern social reformers. We should let the laws of God alone, for we will never discover any better.

5:33–37 *Again, ye have heard that it hath been said by them of old time, Thou shalt not forswear thyself, but shalt perform unto the Lord thine oaths: but I say unto you, Swear not at all; neither by heaven; for it is God's throne: nor by the earth; for it is his footstool: neither by Jerusalem; for it is the city of the great King. Neither shalt thou swear by thy head, because thou canst not make one hair white or black. But let your communication be, Yea, yea; Nay, nay: for whatsoever is more than these cometh of evil.*

False swearing was forbidden of old, but every kind of swearing is forbidden now by the word of our Lord Jesus. He mentions several forms of oaths and forbids them all, and then He dictates simple forms of affirmation or denial, as all that His followers should employ. Notwithstanding much that may be advanced to the contrary, there is no evading the plain sense of this passage, that every sort of oath, however solemn or true, is forbidden to a follower of Jesus. Whether in court of law, or out of it, the rule is, *"Swear not at all."* Yet, in this Christian country we have swearing everywhere, and especially among lawmakers. Our legislators begin their official existence by swearing. By those who obey the law of the Savior's kingdom, all swearing is set aside, that the simple word of affirmation or denial, calmly repeated, may remain as a sufficient bond of truth. A bad man cannot be believed on his oath, and a good man speaks the truth without an oath; to what purpose is the superfluous custom of legal swearing preserved? Christians should not yield to an evil custom, however great the pressure put upon them, but they should abide by the plain and unmistakable command of their Lord and King.

5:38 *Ye have heard that it hath been said, An eye for an eye, and a tooth for a tooth.*

The law of *"an eye for an eye,"* as administered in the proper courts of law, was founded in justice and worked far more equitably than the more modern system of fines, for that latter method allows rich men to offend with comparative impunity. But when *"an eye for an eye"* came to be the rule of daily life, it fostered revenge, and our Savior would not tolerate it as a principle carried out by individuals. Good law in court may be very bad custom in common society. He spoke against what had become a proverb, and was heard and said among the people: *"Ye have heard that it hath been said."*

Our loving King would have private dealings ruled by the spirit of love and not by the rule of law.

5:39 *But I say unto you, That ye resist not evil: but whosoever shall smite thee on thy right cheek, turn to him the other also.*

Nonresistance and forbearance are to be the rule among Christians. They are to endure personal ill-usage without fighting. They are to be like the anvil when bad men are the hammers, and thus they are to overcome by patient forgiveness. The rule of the judgment seat is not for common life, but it is the rule of the cross—and the all-enduring Sufferer is for us all. Yet, how many regard all this as fanatical, utopian, and even cowardly! The Lord, our King, would have us endure and suffer, and then conquer by mighty patience. Can we do it? How are we the servants of Christ if we do not have His Spirit?

5:40 *And if any man will sue thee at the law, and take away thy coat, let him have thy cloak also.*

Let him have all he asks and more. It is better to lose a suit of clothes than be drawn into a suit in law. The courts of our Lord's day were vicious, and His disciples were advised to suffer wrong sooner then appeal to them. Our own courts often furnish the surest method of solving a difficulty by authority, and we have known them resorted to with the purpose of preventing strife. Yet, even in a country where justice can be had, we are not to resort to law for every personal wrong. We should endure being taken advantage of rather than always crying out, "I'll sue you."

At times, this very rule of self-sacrifice may require us to take steps in the way of legal appeal to stop injuries that would fall heavily upon others, but we ought often to forego our own advantage, and do so always, when the main motive would be a proud desire for self-vindication.

Lord, give me a patient spirit, so that I may not seek to avenge myself, even when I might righteously do so!

5:41 *And whosoever shall compel thee to go a mile, go with him twain.*

Governments in those days demanded forced service through their petty officers. Christians were to be of a yielding temper and bear a double exaction rather than provoke ill words and anger. We ought not to evade taxation, but stand ready to render to Caesar his due (Matt. 22:21). "Yield" is our watchword. To stand up against force is not exactly our part; we may leave that to others. How few believe the long-suffering, nonresistant doctrines of our King!

5:42 *Give to him that asketh thee, and from him that would borrow of thee turn not thou away.*

Be generous. A miser is no follower of Jesus. Discretion is to be used in our giving, lest we encourage idleness and beggary, but the general rule is, *"Give to him that asketh thee."* Sometimes a loan may be more useful than a gift; do not refuse it to those who will make the correct use of it. These precepts are not meant for fools. They are set before us as our general rule; but each rule is balanced by other scriptural commands, and there is the teaching of a philanthropic common sense to guide us. The Christian spirit is to be one of readiness to help the needy by gift or loan, and we are not exceedingly likely to err by excess in this direction; hence, the darkness of the command.

5:43 *Ye have heard that it hath been said, Thou shalt love thy neighbour, and hate thine enemy.*

In this case, a command of Scripture had a human antithesis attached to it by depraved minds, and this human addition was mischievous. This is a common method: to append something to the teaching of Scripture that seems to grow out of it or to be a natural inference from it, which may be false and wicked. This is a sad crime against the Word of the Lord. The Holy Spirit will only promote His own words. He owns the precept, *"Thou shalt love thy neighbour,"* but He hates the parasitical growth of *"hate thine enemy."* This last sentence destroys that out of which it appears to grow legitimately, since those who are here presented as enemies are, in fact, neighbors. Love is now the universal law, and our King, who has commanded it, is Himself the Pattern of it. He will not see it narrowed down and placed in a setting of hate. May grace prevent any of us from falling into this error!

5:44-45 *But I say unto you, Love your enemies, bless them that curse you, do good to them that hate you, and pray for them which despitefully use you, and*

*persecute you; that ye may be the children of your Fa-
ther which is in heaven: for he maketh his sun to rise
on the evil and on the good, and sendeth rain on the
just and on the unjust.*

It is ours to persist in loving, even if men persist
in enmity. We are to render blessing for cursing and
prayers for persecutions. In the cases of cruel enemies, we are to *"do good to them...and pray for
them."* We are no longer enemies to any, but friends
to all. We do not merely cease to hate and then abide
in a cold neutrality, but we love where hatred seems
inevitable. We bless where our old nature bids us to
curse, and we are active in doing good to those who
deserve to receive evil from us. Where this is practically carried out, men wonder, respect, and admire
the followers of Jesus. The theory may be ridiculed,
but the practice is reverenced and is counted so sur-
prising that men attribute it to some godlike quality
in Christians, as they acknowledge that they are the
children of the Father who is in heaven. Indeed, he
who can bless the unthankful and the evil is a child
of God, for the Lord is doing this on a great scale in
daily providence, and none but His children will imitate Him.

To do good for the sake of the good done, and
not because of the character of the person benefited,
is a noble imitation of God. If the Lord only sent fer-
tilizing showers upon the land of the saintly,
drought would deprive whole regions of land of all
hope of a harvest. We also must do good for evil, or
we will have a narrow sphere; our hearts will grow
contracted, and our sonship toward the good God
will be rendered doubtful.

5:46 *For if ye love them which love you, what reward have ye? do not even the publicans the same?*

Any common sort of man will love those who love him. Even tax collectors and the scum of the earth can rise to this poor, weak virtue. Saints cannot be content with such a groveling style of things. "Love for love is manlike," but "love for hate" is Christlike. Will we not desire to act according to our high calling?

5:47 *And if ye salute your brethren only, what do ye more than others? do not even the publicans so?*

On a journey, on the streets, or in the house, we are not to confine our friendly greetings to those who are near and dear to us. Courtesy should be wide and nonetheless sincere because general. We should speak kindly to all and treat every man as a brother. Anyone will shake hands with an old friend, but we are to be cordially courteous toward every human being. If not, we will reach no higher level than mere outcasts. Even a dog will salute a dog.

5:48 *Be ye therefore perfect, even as your Father which is in heaven is perfect.*

We should reach after completeness in love and fullness of love to all around us. Love is the bond of being perfect, and if we have perfect love, it will form in us a perfect character. Here is what we aim at: perfection like that of God. Here is the manner of obtaining it: by abounding in love. This suggests the question of how far we have proceeded in this heavenly direction and also the reason why we should persevere in it even to the end, because as children we ought to resemble our Father. Scriptural perfection is attainable; it lies in proportion instead of in degree. A man's character may be perfect and entire, lacking nothing (James 1:4). However, such a man will be the very first to admit that the grace that is in him is at best in its infancy, and though perfect as a child in all its parts, he has not yet attained to the perfection of full-grown manhood.

What a mark is set before us by our Perfect King, who, speaking from His mountain throne, said, *"Be ye therefore perfect, even as your Father which is in heaven is perfect"*! Lord, give what You command; then both the grace and the glory will be Yours alone.

6:1 *Take heed that ye do not your alms before men, to be seen of them: otherwise ye have no reward of your Father which is in heaven.*

This verse is saying, "You cannot expect to be paid twice. If, therefore, you take your reward in the applause of men, who give you a high character for generosity, you cannot then expect to have any reward from God." We ought to have a single focus on God's accepting what we give, and to have little or no thought of what man may say concerning our charitable gifts.

6:2 *Therefore when thou doest thine alms, do not sound a trumpet before thee, as the hypocrites do in the synagogues and in the streets, that they may have* *glory of men. Verily I say unto you, They have their reward.*

And they will have no more. There is, in their cases, no laying up of any store of good works before God. Whatever they may have done, they have taken full credit for it in the praise of men.

6:3 *But when thou doest alms, let not thy left hand know what thy right hand doeth.*

This verse is saying, "Do it so by stealth, as scarcely to know of it yourself. Think so little of it with regard to yourself that you will scarcely know that you have done it. Do it unto God; let Him know it."

6:4 *That thine alms may be in secret: and thy Father which seeth in secret himself shall reward thee openly.*

There is a blessed emphasis upon that word *"himself,"* for, if God will reward us, what a reward it will be! Any praise from His lips, any reward from His hands, will be of priceless value. Oh, to live with an eye to that alone!